The Guinea Pig

Edmundo Morales

The Guinea Pig

Healing, Food, and Ritual in the Andes

The University of Arizona Press   Tucson

The University of Arizona Press
Copyright © 1995
Arizona Board of Regents
All Rights Reserved

♾ This book is printed on acid-free,
archival-quality paper. Manufactured
in the United States of America.

00 99 98 97 96 95
6 5 4 3 2 1

Library of Congress Cataloging-in-
Publication Data will be found at the
end of this book.

To my sons, Angel and Edmundo, Jr.,

who, I hope, will seek their roots through my work.

They more than anyone else know that this book

is the result of my long journey from my native home in the Andes

to my adopted hometown in the United States, the Big Apple.

Contents

Illustrations

Acknowledgments

Fieldwork to research this book was funded by the American Philosophical Society in 1990, a Faculty Development award of West Chester University in 1991, and a Fulbright research award in 1992. During collection of data for writing this book, I was fortunate to meet people who were helpful with their criticism, encouragement, and guidance. Each person with whom I spoke about my project contributed to the fulfilling of a dream that had lingered in my mind since my days as a graduate student. My wife, Norma, had the strength to stay back home with our two sons while I spent many months in the field. She gave me moral support, tolerated my piles of folders, papers, and books in the house, and patiently took most of the burdens of the housework while I was away in the field or working at home. My two sons, Angel and Edmundo, endured my five years of nomadic academic life; despite their young age, they understood that everything I did was because of my love for them—even though I spent three consecutive summers away from them. This work cannot justify the memorable moments in their lives I missed during my absence.

I am indebted to many other people. My mother, Felicitas Bayona, my brothers Edinson, David, and Cesar, and my sister Adelaida and her husband, Juan, helped me during fieldwork in Peru. My thanks to Peter J. Harris for his continued, unconditional support and for graciously securing many dozens of packs of Polaroid film that I used in the field; to Wayne Geist for developing many rolls of film and for printing my contact sheets; to Bill Kornblum for being supportive of my work since my first semester as a graduate student; to Jack Kloppenburg, Paul Stoller, and Steven King for their recommendations to make my project fundable; to Wolfgang Schüler for inviting me to join him in his photographic expedition in the summer of 1990.

I am also grateful to the researchers of the Instituto Nacional de Investigación Agraria in Lima, Peru, especially Lilia Chauca and her late husband Marco Zaldívar for their help in 1990; to Alberto Caycedo, Gerardo Montenegro, Segundo Burbano, and Alberto Campaña in Pasto, Colombia, for their assistance in 1994; to Hermilio Rosas of the Museo Nacional de Arqueología y Antropología in Lima, Peru; to Sor Aida Cisneros of the Convento de San Diego in Quito and the Ecuador-España Cultural Project in Ecuador for allowing me to photograph their collections; to Catalina Amuy and her daughters Sonia, Miriam, and Ketty in Lima for always having a room available upon my unexpected arrivals; to Marcelino Espinoza, Ciro and Paco García, Dina Sotomayor de Vidal and her family in Llamellín, Ancash, Peru, for their thoughtful attention; to Valdi and Elena Fischer and their family for sharing the intimacy of their home with me; and to Neils Noya and his family in Bolivia, Nelson and Isabel Vallejo, Felix and Dunia Paladines, Kelvi Heredia, and Jean de Neef in Ecuador for their warmhearted hospitality.

Finally, I am indebted to the staff of the Fulbright Commission in Ecuador, especially Gonzalo Cartagenova and Helena Saona, for making my fieldwork in 1992 an exciting and profitable stay; to Enrique Mayer, Roberto Moncayo, and Braulio Muñoz for their valuable comments to help clarify some ideas and interpretations; to Regina Harrison for helping me visit areas in the countryside of Ecuador that I would not have seen on my own; to Victoria, Barbara, and Leigh Shaffer for making me feel at home away from home during my move from New York to Pennsylvania; to Richard Brand for his efforts to make my work known to policymakers; to Daniel Yeh for his prompt and courteous service during the initial literature search; to Linda B. Malik for her diligent and prompt proofreading of the galleys; to Carolina Lutterman, Jodie Hawkins, Joan Smith, Karen Secrist, and Emily Balzano for their exceptional secretarial work; to Leonard and Evelyn Ratner for continuing to take care of my apartment in New York City; to Bill Berger and the late Joe Berthe for helping me with their kind and generous, humanistic deeds. Last but not least, my thanks to Victor Hasselblad, Inc., for furnishing basic equipment and accessories that allowed me to take advantage of the superb Hasselblad system to photograph on three fieldtrips.

Introduction

Recently in a suburb of New York City, an Andean immigrant decided to raise guinea pigs on his property, and for that purpose he built a room that would be similar to a thatched kitchen in a house if he still lived in the Andes. His intention was to have guinea pig meat available for special occasions and summer barbecues. On warm days in the spring he grazed his animals on his half acre of property. One afternoon he forgot to feed the guinea pigs and failed to shut them in the room in which they lived. He was unaware that guinea pigs eat twenty-four hours a day and do not sleep. He did not expect the guinea pigs to wander into the thick grass of his large yard. The animals were unable to find their way back to their domicile, and when the temperature dropped acutely that night they were without shelter. The next morning to the man's dismay all twenty guinea pigs had died of hypothermia.

In the United States, the guinea pig (*Cavia porcellus*) is most familiar as a common pet for young children. But today in New York City, one can frequent any of a number of ethnic restaurants and find guinea pig offered as an entrée. Even street food vendors sell roasted guinea pigs in some parts of the city, and Andean immigrants barbecue guinea pig meat in public parks the way Americans would hamburgers or hot dogs. While the guinea pig in its native environment has traditionally been raised for consumption, it also has had important ceremonial uses in folk medicine and in native religious practices. Nevertheless, because of its high protein content, the guinea pig is becoming a valued market commodity in the Andes and throughout the world (Morales 1994). Latin

Americans are raising guinea pigs commercially for the first time as a means of supplementing their incomes, while traditionally the animals remain an important part of cultural rituals.

This book is specifically about the traditional cultural uses of the guinea pig in the Andes of Bolivia, Colombia, Ecuador, and Peru, and therefore I will hereafter refer to it by its Spanish name, *cuy*. I intend to convey an understanding of the role the cuy plays in traditions and behaviors of Andeans and at the same time to shed light on national and international policies of economic development that conflict with the values of most Andean populations. This study of culture change will be useful for social scientists, humanists, and policymakers, as well as the general public.

At this point, because I know firsthand how important the cuy is in the Andes, and perhaps to defend it from those who would simply label it as an exotic aberration of my culture, I want briefly to present my own background as a member of the culture under study.

I was born and raised in a small town of about 2,500 people, far in the northeastern Andes of Peru. Until I was fourteen years old, I had never seen a road or a car. When I left home for Lima in the spring of 1956, I hiked for about twelve hours to reach the road. I remember my mother telling me that when she was a child the same trip could take as long as two weeks on foot and that people would take along well-spiced fried cuys to eat while they traveled. Some of the commodities we used from the outside world when I was growing up were sugar, salt, spices, kerosene, wax candles, and some piece goods for clothing. People had to travel for two or three days to acquire these goods and then transport them back home on donkeys. We had plenty of food, wheat, barley, quinua (*Chenopodium quinua*), corn, and potatoes, as well as other Andean tubers. We made our own bread because we even had water mills where we took our grains to have them ground.

The closest hospital, which most people either could not afford or refused to use, was about fifteen hours by horseback, or longer on foot, from my hometown. The use of plants and animals made up the first and foremost method of curing illnesses and diseases. I remember an eight-year-old boy who had a bad case of pimples on his scalp. His mother tried to cure him by using herbs and plants, all of which proved ineffective. The local midwife suggested that she wash the boy's hair with a brown soap that was known to be strong and then rinse it with fermented urine every other day.[1] The combination of the strong soap and urine caused the boy excruciating pain, but after about three weeks of this treatment the boy's scalp healed. As recently as the early eighties I have also observed that many people drink their own fresh, warm urine to cure colic when outside help is not available.

Dental hygiene was also a matter of self-treatment when I was growing up. Salt rocks and coca leaves were used as toothache relievers. Since no dentist lived in town, or even nearby, tooth extraction procedures were cruel and traumatic, to say the least. Every time I go to my dentist I think of the time of my first tooth extraction when I was about eight years old. My left premolar was decayed, and ached so badly that I banged my head against the wall and begged my mother to do something about it. The most immediate help in town was Lucio Tarazona, the only local tinsmith who was known for being a good *saca muela* (tooth puller). When my mother and I arrived at the smith's house, he was struggling to extract the decayed tooth of an older boy. I was terrified when I saw Lucio fail a second time to pull the tooth. When my mother read my face she grabbed my hands tightly so that I could not run away. The smith pulled the boy's tooth in his third attempt, after which he took a brief break. Now it was my turn, and Lucio assured me that he would spare me the pain the other boy had gone through. He asked me to lie on a thick sheepskin placed on the ground and then summoned his wife who folded a light woolen quilt upon which I rested my head. He instructed his wife to have a cup of brine ready. Lucio's wife held my legs, and my mother pressed my arms. The smith kept my mouth open with his left hand, placed his right knee on my chest, grabbed a pair of thin pliers, and pulled my decayed tooth on the first try. I rinsed my mouth with brine until the bleeding stopped. Lucio rarely recommended taking over-the-counter analgesics. Rather, if there was any swelling, he prescribed application of slices of black potato or fresh, black clay on the face.

In October 1966, when my town became the capital of the new province of Antonio Raimondi, a road was built, thus simplifying people's connection to the outside world and ultimately making them dependent on that world. The most immediate effects of modernization were the changes in the people's consumer behavior. Truckers brought flour from Lima to make bread. Occasionally, people even consumed potatoes imported from Europe. Thus, an area which had known a way of life based on subsistence agriculture became part of a market economy without having developed the resources, such as higher forms of education, that would satisfy the technical needs that came with modernization. A trained dentist opened his office in a town that was about five hours walking distance, and people from my town used his services. In the early seventies, about two hundred meters from Lucio Tarazona's house, the government built a medical post where an intern from a dental school in Lima and two nurses rendered services to those who decided to try modern, scientific medicine. One extreme case I witnessed was of a person with pneumonia who had not been cured with the traditional medical practice of rubbing the patient's back with warm chicken or cuy fat.

Andean culture has changed in other ways since I was a boy. Two folk practices out of many others that have already disappeared are of particular interest to me. Until the late sixties, during two *aya tapay* (wake) nights after a death, groups of local boys improvised a frolic called *llatino*. The play was designed to comfort mourners and entertain people who came to the wake. The head of the llatino was always an experienced man who had either been a relative or had known the deceased well. Depending on the dead person's popularity or social status in the community, the number of the llatinos could range from five to as many as thirty boys. Each and every llatino would roll his poncho, tie it on his back, and cover his face with the brim of his hat to remain anonymous. The group, in single file following the leader's chanting instructions, would burst into the house of mourners and charge at people, especially women sitting on benches, agave tree stools, and on the ground by the door of the room where the coffin was. The leader would issue commands to his followers in Quechua. For example, before coming to the wake, the llatino group would go to the community faucet or to the nearest spring to fill their mouths with water. Upon the leader's chanting command *ishpakachellapa* ("now let us all urinate"), the llatinos would squirt the water from their mouths onto the people. Also at the leader's command "let us now pick and touch our girl," the llatinos would touch women who then giggled and tried to identify the llatinos. For some llatinos this frolic was a match-making ritual. The llatino who had identified the girl he liked would try to take away some possession belonging to the girl, such as a ring, a kerchief, or a hat. If the girl did not recover her personal belonging, the understanding was that she would consent to the beginning of a romance, or even a sexual encounter. For other males, the llatino was an opportunity to see their girlfriends, or their mistresses, if they were married. At the end of the frolic, the mourning family would serve the llatinos hot meals, such as diced potato soup and coffee, in a room separate from the wake or in a corner of the house.

If the aya tapay was for a baby or a child younger than seven years (also known as *parvulo tapay*) the wake was a party, rather than an occasion to grieve. Families and relatives entertained people who came to the wake and provided music, drinks, and food. The parents would invite a musician or a group of musicians to play for one night. Friends, neighbors, and relatives would contribute drinks and chicken or cuy to be slaughtered for the parvulo tapay night. The rationale for the parvulo party was that a baby or a child departed for afterlife without having sinned, which merited celebration rather than grief. Today, the parvulo party is still observed in some isolated communities in the northeastern Andes of Peru.

Another folk practice with which I became familiar is an erotic play called *chuchunacuy*, literally translated as "to breast-feed each other," but actually meaning "to play with the breasts." During the month of February single women, especially shepherds, grazed their flocks as far as three to four hours walking distance from their communities. During this month the traditional *millkapa* (snack), which always consisted of toasted maize or baked potatoes or ocas (*Oxalis tuberosa*), also included fried ham or cuy. In some instances young women organized a "cookout" for which they took with them clay pots, frying pans, and food such as cuys, pigeons, eggs, and potatoes to cook. Women stood on the tops of hills and mountains and sang provocative ballads called *arawi* as loud and as many times as it was necessary for them to catch the attention of boys and men from nearby villages or towns. The arawi's lyric was an improvisation, which was not uniform, and it always contained Quechua words for flowers and parts of the human body. An eighty-year-old woman from the high punas once simulated for me the arawi that she had sung so many times. First she hummed and then uttered the Quechua words for hair, hands, legs, breasts, and flowers, such as a white lily, rose, carnation, and some wild flowers native to the Cordilleras. She ended the lyric with the words *pukllallay* (dare playing with them), which would entice young men to come and play.

Upon hearing the arawi, males, usually matching the number of females, got together to hike up to the hills and plateaus in the punas. The young women stopped singing the arawi as soon as they sighted their play partners and huddled on the ground and tried to figure out the young men's identities and marital status, and then evaluate their physical looks and stamina, and so forth. Once the men came to the spot where the women were huddling, the women would spread out and begin running away from the men. The challenge for the men was to catch the women and play the chuchunacuy, which consisted in a man's wrestling a woman to the ground and rubbing her breasts with his chin. This erotic folk play almost always ended in coitus and pregnancy, which increased the number of illegitimate children in the Andes. Informants tell of occasions when, in order to subdue women for a "comfortable chuchunacuy," men would tie the women's hands behind their backs, especially if the women were stronger or did not cooperate with their male partners when forced to the ground. In some instances a woman would actually knock a man out, in which cases the other men ridiculed him for not having succeeded in the play. According to Bernabe Cobo, chuchunacuy may have been one of the sexual initiation rituals during which women "consented to be deflowered because they wanted to be free of the shame which the chaste had to endure simply for being 'virgins.'"[2] Introduction of the concept of the Virgin Mary during colonial times as the model for the ideal woman may have changed the Indians' attitudes toward sex. Thus chuchunacuy may have originally been a clandestine transitional rite of passage from puberty to adulthood. Today, llatino and chuchunacuy, as well as many other folk plays, rites, and romps, have either changed substantially or disappeared altogether.

The Cuy in Andean Culture

The high-protein, low-fat content of cuy meat makes it a desirable commodity among non-native as well as native populations. For this reason the scientific community became interested in and succeeded in finding a means of breeding cuys that offered more meat faster than the traditional method of breeding. The pattern is a familiar one, the same as in the commercial exploitation of other natural resources: populations that have preserved the cuy germ plasm for centuries will most likely lose control of it, and the significant cultural traditions that have grown around the cuy will be lost to the capitalist economy. Neglect of agriculture by the highland population and the growing dependence on urban areas will, in the long run, transform the uses to which cuy are put. The change of the place of the cuy within Andean culture will affect traditions and religious practices, which will then be replaced by more modern behaviors. Within a foreseeable future cuys used in traditional practices and rituals may come from commercial farms. Because the cuy is an integral part of the Andean culture, its origin is critical to the authenticity of rituals. The use of cuy from outside the culture will break the Andean man's tie to his ecology, and the rituals surrounding the cuy will lose their social meaning.

The drive to integrate indigenous peoples into the modern market economy has led Latin American governments to implement development policies that are aggressively changing traditions and values in the Andes. To cite one example, Bolivian, Ecuadorian, and Peruvian governments have tried to develop the countryside by advancing education and motorized transportation in the hinterland and by opening new agricultural enterprises, mostly in the rain forests. These efforts by governing officials have spawned migration shifts from the highlands to urban areas, have encouraged peasants' participation in the informal economy (de Soto 1989), and have facilitated their making connections to the international, informal underground cocaine economy (Lee 1989; Morales 1989; Malamud 1992; Sanabria 1993). It is not unrealistic to predict that drastic changes in the traditional culture will take place within the next few decades. Traditional ways of life merit a comprehensive, firsthand documentation and interpretation, because the drive to modernize indigenous groups will, undoubtedly, decimate these traditions and customs. It is important to document the various uses of the cuy while the environment still flourishes and people still have the same social practices.

Colonial chroniclers and many contemporary archaeologists and anthropologists mention the cuy in their works, but a study of the animal as an important element in Andean culture has not been done. With only three journal articles and one book in Spanish, the paucity of literature on the cuy in the Andean culture and society becomes obvious. Bolton's (1979) argument that there is a link between seasonal consumption of cuy meat at religious festivities and the production cycle of the cuy, and that religious occasions are an excuse for protein intake may not hold true even in the small community in southeastern Peru where he collected his data.

The place of the cuy in human ecology (Gade 1967) is changing. People who raise cuys in the kitchen and observe particular folk practices pertaining to its use (Escobar and Escobar 1976) are prejudged to be antiquated and backward. The best ethnographic work on the cuy (Archetti 1992) is limited to Ecuador and falls short of being the comprehensive study that is needed.

Although my book focuses on the cultural significance of the cuy, it also attempts as an ethnographic work to provide a holistic presentation of everyday life in the Andes. It says a lot about families, children, household economy, food practices, symbols, politics, and social structure. At the same time, it reports the participation of both Andean and non-Andean people in the modern cuy economy. It concludes that the cuy may be on its way to becoming yet another exploited natural resource. This knowledge will raise questions about the ethicality of biotechnological research that breeds bigger cuys for the benefit of urban populations. Awareness of the problems will perhaps encourage academics to do more research on the social and psychological consequences to ethnic populations brought about by commercialization of a natural resource. Optimistically, the study should help policymakers to realize that knowledge of indigenous peoples and their cultural practices must be included in the overall plan of economic development.

About three decades ago, a group of agronomists in Lima, Peru, embarked on a research project that totally changed the place of the cuy in the Andes, as well as its role in regional economies. The hypothesis of the research was that in-breeding resulting from raising cuys in the kitchens of individuals' homes was causing new generations of cuys to be smaller in size. Today, the promotion of controlled breeding and subsequent increase in the numbers of cuys available have encouraged people to explore this new way of earning a living and of supplementing their traditionally very low intake of protein.

By and large, even discounting family consumption of cuy, the demand for the meat is higher than the available supply. For the individual Andean, however, success at cuy farming as the sole source of income depends on a combination of factors, such as the amount of capital available, a willingness to take a risk, organization, technology, and entrepreneurial vision, to name a few. These prerequisites are often absent among groups in Andean society who, in many ways, are still accustomed to paternalistic policies. Entrepreneurs who grab the opportunity at either end of the cuy economy—production or consumption—are pioneers. The classic example of production is Roberto Moncayo, an Ecuadorian agronomist who owns and operates the largest cuy farm in the world. Ten years ago he invested about U.S. $350,000 to get set up in business. He now enjoys a profit of about U.S. $50,000 per year, lives a comfortable middle-class life, and invests in the national stock market thanks to his success in cuy agribusiness.[3]

While readers may view my photographs as celebrations of the Andean culture, my intention is to try to help them better understand the link between traditions of the past and present practices, and to document what remains of the Andean culture. The purpose of this book is to demonstrate how microcosmic settings in the Andes are perceived and experienced. I believe this book fulfills these purposes by offering the reader personal and human profiles of behavior on all the aspects of the use of the cuy on which I collected data.

Chapter 1 presents the biological and historical characteristics of the cuy. It also documents social practices of cuy raising and discusses how the cuy is scientifically bred. Finally, it addresses commercial production and marketing of the cuy. The focus of chapter 2 is the use of the cuy as a symbol to bind social contracts and reciprocities and thus to preserve the indigenous culture.[4] The last two

chapters deal with the Andean worldview and native religious beliefs and practices. Descriptions and sociological interpretations of
the use of the cuy in the celebration of local religious events connected to the Catholic faith are examined. The concluding chapter
connects the cuy as an Andean legacy to the major social, economic,
and political dilemmas that the Andes is facing today.

The settings for this study were numerous communities in the
highlands of Bolivia, Colombia, Ecuador, and Peru. The first phase
of the fieldwork took place in the summer of 1990 in Bolivia and
southeastern Peru; the second phase, conducted in 1991, covered
central and northern Peru; the third phase in 1992 included the
highlands of Ecuador; and the fourth phase was concluded in
southern Colombia in the summer of 1994. I entered the world
of the participant(s) as it was and obtained data without any delib-
erate intention of altering the setting. At the outset of the actual
data collection, I practiced my customary "familiarization walk"
around the setting (Morales 1989:175). This candid tour around
the community opened doors to informal, general conversations
with identified or potential subjects. Because many people in highland communities selected for the study did not speak Spanish,
and inasmuch as the use of the native language facilitated data
collection, I used primarily the Quechua language in every possible situation. In some places and areas, however, I could hardly
communicate with people because so many different dialects are
spoken.

My participation in civil and religious events brought me in
contact with people from neighboring communities or people
who otherwise may have been difficult to meet—people such as
folk doctors, witches, and midwives. My social traits, my communication skills, and my experience in collecting data in unusual
situations simplified my entrée to and rapport with the communities selected for the study. My participant-observer role followed
two strategies: total participant and researcher-participant (Gans
1986:54). My total participation entailed emotional involvement
in events and situations featuring the use of the cuy. My researcher-
participant, or indirect role, implied watching and recording the
external demonstrations of the festivities and rituals. The body of
the data comes from field notes, as well as taped conversations and
discussions with key informants.

It was my practice in doing fieldwork to take notes immediately after observation and not to tape subjects unless I was authorized to do so. I used in the field about 800 sheets of instant Polaroid film, primarily for exposure and composition tests. But having instant pictures to share also eased entrée to and rapport with some groups and individuals, and in some cases led to conversations from which I was able to gather additional information that might otherwise have been difficult or impossible to obtain. A detailed discussion of the methodology used during fieldwork appears in the appendix.

The Guinea Pig

Chapter One

From Household Animal
to Market Commodity

In South America, plants such as the potato (*Solanum tuberosum*) and quinua (*Chenopodium quinua*), and animals such as the llama (*Lama glama*) and cuy are widely used as sources of food. According to the Peruvian archaeologist Lumbreras (1981:135–141 and 1983:40), domestication of the cuy, along with plants and other animals in the Andes, may have begun about 5000 B.C. in the Altiplano area where the wild cuy (*Cavia aparera*), known as quita k'owi in Bolivia and as ulluay in Cajamarca, Peru, still exists today.[1] The cuy may have been extensively eaten along with shellfish and other fish on the Pacific Coast. Indeed, existence of statues representing cuys from the Moche Valley around A.D. 1400 in Peru and archaeological evidence in the province of Manabí, Ecuador, around 500 B.C. to A.D. 500 indicate that the cuy was raised and used on the coast (Stahl and Norton 1984:88).

The cuy is a misnamed animal, for it is neither a pig, nor is it from Guinea. It may not even be a member of the rodent family.[2] One possible explanation of this misnomer may be that guinea is a corruption of Guiana, the South American country from which cuys may have been exported. Europeans may also have thought that cuys came from the West African coast of Guinea, for they may have been imported from South America via the Guinea slave trade ships. Another possibility is that cuys were sold for one guinea each in England. A guinea was a gold coin issued there in 1663. All over Europe cuys became popular as pets; Queen Elizabeth I herself had one and therefore helped to contribute to this pet fancy (MAG 1986). Although most people from the Andes call the guinea pig "cuy," the Aymaras know it as *wanku* and *wankuchi*. In many parts of Bolivia cuy is known as *conejo cui* (rabbit cuy), *conejo peruano* (Peruvian rabbit), or *conejo nativo* (native rabbit). In southern Colombia, it is known as *curi* and *huimbo*, *cobayo* or *huiro*; in Venezuela as *acurito*; and in Cuba as *curiel*. In some parts of the Andes of Peru it takes the Quechua name of *jaca* (pronounced haka) or *aca*, or *sacca* (Junín), and *quwi* or *qowa* in Cuzco. In Ecuador, people think that cuy is a Quechua word.[3] Although the cuy's natural habitat is the Andes from northern Chile to southern Colombia, today scientifically bred cuys from Peru have been introduced into other countries such as the highlands of Honduras, the Dominican Republic, and many other parts of the world (Chauca and Zaldívar 1989). Researchers call the breeding of Peruvian male cuys with indigenous female cuys *mestizaje*. Chauca (1993:3) claims that the mestizo cuy has a higher food conversion rate and makes faster ecological adaptation than its parent cuys.

Chauca (1993:33) reports that in Peru, according to the Ministry of Agriculture, there are about 22 million cuys. Scientists at the Instituto Nacional de Investigación Agraria (INIA) calculate,

Statue of a *cuy* from the Mochica-Chimu pre-Inca culture on the Pacific coast of Peru.

A scientifically bred, six-month-old cuy. Small-headed, short-haired, and light-colored cuys are the most desirable animals to raise for their meat.

however, that there are at least 30 million cuys in Peru.[4] In Ecuador the number of cuys is estimated at well over 10 million (MAG 1986; Moncayo 1992a).[5] In Colombia, Montenegro (1993:183) argues that there are at least 700,000 cuys, almost 29 percent more than Koeslag's (1989:22) calculation.[6] In Bolivia, where the cuy is found throughout the country, the number of cuys may be well over 3 million. Thus, the cuy germ plasm is an Andean legacy.

The average cuy weighs about 0.75 kilograms. The average length of an adult cuy is about 30 cm, the smallest being about 20 cm and the largest about 40 cm. The cuy has no tail. The pelage can be smooth or coarse, short or long, and it is curly in some varieties. The most common colors are white, dark brown, gray, and combinations of these colors. Black is the rarest color. The cuy is extremely prolific. Female cuys become pregnant at the age of three months, and every sixty-five to seventy-five days thereafter.[7] The period of estrus is from thirteen to twenty-four days and lasts for seven to eight hours. Post parturition estrus, which takes place three or four hours after delivery and every seventeen days thereafter, is a characteristic of the cuy. About 78 percent of females that

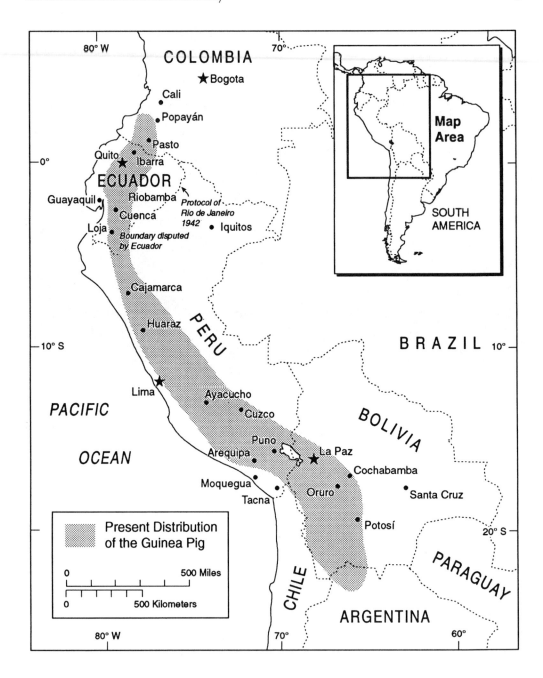

exhibit post parturition estrus become pregnant (Aliaga 1989). Although they have only two dugs, cuys can feed litters of five to six pups without any difficulty because of the high fat content of the milk they produce (see Table 1.1).

The average number of pups per litter is two to four, but litters of up to eight pups are not uncommon (Aliaga 1989). Cuys can

live as long as nine years, but the average lifespan is three years. Seven females can produce as many as seventy-two offspring a year, yielding a net amount of more than thirty-five kilograms of meat (Charbonneau 1988:7). Research demonstrates that the Peruvian cuys bred with the indigenous (*criollo*) cuys weigh about 850 grams three months after birth and can adapt more quickly to different environments than the indigenous or criollo cuys (Chauca 1993a:3) (see Table 1.2).[8] Given ideal conditions, a farmer starting with one male and ten females could see his flock grow to 361 animals in one year.[9] Farmers who raise cuys for the market dispose of reproducing females following the third litter because these females grow big, weighing well over 1.2 kilos, and sell faster and for higher prices than male cuys or unreproductive female cuys of the same age; the number of offspring in the fourth litter is no greater than that of the second or third litter; reproduc-

One square meter is the average size of a cuy breeding box. Each box has ten females and one male, but in some cases farmers put as many as twelve females in a single box. The cuys pictured here are all dark brown.

Table 1.1   Comparison of Cuy Milk to Other Mammals

Animal	Water (%)	Albumins (%)	Fat (%)	Salts (%)
Cuy	41.10	11.20	46.0	0.57
Cow	86.00	3.80	3.7	0.65
Mare	89.00	2.70	1.6	0.51
Human	87.00	1.10	4.5	0.20

Source: MAG (Ministerio de Agricultura y Ganadería) (1986:7)

ing females consume more feed than other cuys of comparable age; and the mortality rate for mother cuys after the third litter is higher (Moncayo 1992a).

Cuys are extremely adaptable to the temperate zones of the highland tropics and high mountains, but they are usually kept indoors to protect them from the extremes of weather. Although they can be raised at temperatures as high as 30°C, the natural habitat seems to be places where temperatures fluctuate from 22°C in the daytime to −7°C at night. Cuys, however, cannot survive freezing temperatures and may not perform well when exposed to the full tropical heat and sunlight (NRC 1991:244). Because of its adaptability to different altitudes, the cuy is found in areas as low as the Amazon Basin rain forests and as high as the *punas* (cold, arid regions at high altitudes). The cuy's physical adaptability allows the commercial farmer or family to feed a flock with forage available in the environment to which the cuy has adapted. Throughout the Andes almost every family has at least twenty cuys. About 90 percent of the total population of cuys in the Andes is produced within the traditional household (Moncayo 1992a). The kitchen is the proper place to keep cuys; some people have cubbyholes or hutches, *cuyeros* in Spanish or *jacapukus* in Quechua, built with adobe bricks or reed and clay, or in small hutlike kitchens without windows. Cuys are always running about the floor, especially when they are hungry. Some people believe that cuys need smoke, which is why they keep them in the kitchen. Although alfalfa (*Medicago sativa*) is their favorite feed, they are fed on table scraps such as potato peelings, carrots, grass, fresh corncobs, and grains. In some areas of Peru during the dry season *retama* (*Spartium junceum*) is the most frequent feed used (Chauca 1993:2). At low altitudes, where

A room in Salasaca, Ecuador, that is used as a kitchen and a bedroom.

banana agriculture is the main economic activity, cuys are fed with ripe bananas. Cuys start eating forage or balanced feed a few hours after birth. Mother's milk is a supplement, not part of the main diet.[10] They get their supply of water from the forage. Farmers who feed their cuys with concentrated feed have their own system of providing water.

This woman in Bolivia keeps her cuys in a two-story adobe cage. She is culling cuys to send them to a local restaurant.

Table 1.2 Comparison of Criollo, Mestizo, and Peruvian Cuys In the Province of Pichincha, Ecuador

	Genetic Line		
	Criollo	Peruvian	Mestizo
Pups per liter	1.44	2.22	1.90
Weight at birth	127.31 kilos	145.75	137.63
Weight at 3 weeks	257.69	298.88	288.42
Weight at 3 months	637.69	853.89	847.79

Source: Olivio Silva, MAG, Conocoto, Quito, Ecuador. In Chauca (1993a:3)

In the Cuzco region people believe that *sutuchi* (remainder of corn used to make chicha) is the best feed (Escobar and Escobar 1976:40). When cuys are fed they rest in the corners, inside clay pots sitting on the floor, or by the hearth. The flock of cuys gives the kitchen and the household a special characteristic to such a point that people who do not have cuys in their kitchen are stereotyped as lazy or extremely poor. People say of such a person, "*allau-*

chi jacampich kanchu," meaning "I feel so sorry for him because he does not even have a single cuy." Many families who live at high altitudes usually share their house with their cuys (Weismantel 1988:101). Thus the cuy is a significant ingredient in the household, and the raising of it, as well as its consumption as meat, influences the folklore, ideology, language, and the household economy.

By nature, Andeans are attached to their animals because they share space in the house and because they invest time and energy to care for them. They treat big work animals like pets and often name them after plants, flowers, natural forces, and mountains. Chickens and cuys, however, are rarely named. They are identified by their own physical characteristics such as color of pelage or feathers, sex, size, or combinations of these characteristics.

Raising of cuy is still part of the Andean folk culture. The first reproductive specimens usually come to the household as gifts or through exchange; people rarely buy them. Women who go to visit relatives and friends, or children who go with their fathers to the field to work, sometimes bring back a gift, which in many

This building of brick is a cuy room constructed with funds provided by the Belgian government in Imbabura, Ecuador.

The family in Pesillo, Ecuador, who owns this cuy room has maximized available space by building two-story cuy boxes.

instances is a chicken or a cuy. Friends and relatives commonly give children cuys as treats or because they may be reciprocating some earlier gift they received from the parents and therefore are paying them back. Perhaps the cuy is given as advance payment for some favor to be asked at a later date. A child may get a cuy from a fictive kin (*madrina* or *padrino*) simply as a present. The cuy that is given as a gift becomes part of the family's already existing flock, if there is one. If the cuy is the first one in a family and is a female that is at least three months old, it is highly likely to be pregnant. If not, a male cuy is borrowed or rented from a neighbor or relative. If the male cuy is rented, the owner is always paid in kind, the value depending on the male's breed. The owner of the cuy that is rented out may demand a female puppy from the first litter or another male puppy to be consumed in any upcoming ceremony or social event. The borrowed male is returned as soon as another male reaches mating age.

The various tasks involved in raising cuys are performed traditionally by women and children in conjunction with their other household tasks. When boys, girls, or women who tend animals, for instance, bring lunch for men who are hoeing a corn plot, they always collect feed for the cuys. It is common to see women and children carrying on their backs scraps, corncobs, or husks for their household animals. Children who come back from the field without some firewood or feed for cuys are scolded for being lazy or negligent. Cleaning the kitchen floor or the cuy cubby holes is also part of women's and children's work.

In many communities, children claim ownership of puppies. If two puppies are of the same color or sex, they mark their choices by cleaving or piercing one ear or marking them in ink or by some other method. Once the puppies are claimed, the owner can dispose of the cuy as he or she pleases. The claimed cuy can be exchanged, borrowed, sold, or slaughtered. This practice functions something like petty cash for women or allowance or tips for children for carrying out their chores properly. Thus, a schoolchild may one day decide to sell his or her cuy for cash or offer it to his godparent, or give it to a community cause. This type of ownership is also true for other small household animals. Claims of ownership of animals used in agriculture and transportation are decided or settled by parents, usually fathers.

Traditionally, the cuy was raised exclusively as a source of meat for consumption on special ceremonial occasions or events, not as daily or even weekly sources of meat. It is only recently that households have begun giving the cuy exchange value. The use value, however, still predominates. If, because of scarcity of feed or because of recent civil or religious ceremonial obligations, a family is unable to serve cuy to a distinguished guest or a relative visiting from a faraway place, chicken is substituted for cuy. In this case, the host family may plead to be excused for not being able to offer what the occasion deserves. It should be underscored that in many instances when cuys are slaughtered, members of the household, especially women and children, are served last, and only if there is enough meat. They usually end up nibbling the head or the inner organs or fried blood served with boiled potatoes. Hence, the cuy's special role is to save face for the family, so to speak, or to avoid criticism by visitors, neighbors, and the community.

The cuy's influence and presence in Andean society goes beyond its ceremonial role. The cuy is used as a common comparative. For instance, someone might liken a woman who has too many children to a cuy, or make jokes about women who stop having children being sterile because "they do not have sexual intercourse following their last child delivery." In other instances, people who do not want to hire someone who is reputed to be lazy or unskilled say that "he is not good even for tending cuys" (el no sirve ni para cuidar cuys), meaning that he is unable to perform even the simplest task. Women and children who want to leave their communities to travel to the city ask truckers, itinerant merchants, or visitors, "Please take me along that I may be useful at least to give your cuys water." The use of the word cuy is even found in the lyrics of folk songs, such as "Hey old lady, if you want me to be your son-in-law, open your door and serve me a whole cuy" in Quechua.

Not long ago, in the folk culture, hiding or stealing small animals was not defined as a misdemeanor. Rather, it was a mere travesura (prank), and sometimes young boys would be known by their travesuras. Thus, a boy who had stolen cuys would be known as jaca sua (cuy stealer) in Quechua, or as a weasel. Boys would steal cuys, chickens, and eggs, usually from their own houses, and the stolen items would be used to cook during one-day trips (paseos) or at group feasts or parties for which boys would provide meat, spices, and firewood. Girls would "borrow" pots, dishes, and other wares from their houses to cook a dish or dishes that the group had planned. If the travesura involved stealing cuys or chickens from other people in the community, and if the traviesos (mischievous boys) were caught, parents always took responsibility for paying for the travesura of their children. In some cases the targets for the travesuras were the kitchens of religious officers who were raising or keeping cuys and chickens for ceremonial meals.

In December of 1954 a group of six boys, including myself, and two girls (sisters) decided to cook in the house of the two girls whose parents were out of town. The purpose was to have a feast to celebrate the local patron saint's day a few days before the actual date. Two boys in the group were from a small town about six hours walking distance, and they were attending school in my hometown. Four of us (the two outsiders and two local boys) were asked to provide the group with no less than four cuys, for our goal was to eat at least half a cuy each, something that we had not yet experienced. The two outsiders were unable to steal from the house in which they were boarding, and the two local boys' kitchens had very few cuys so that if one or two were stolen, their parents would have aborted our plan. The four of us decided to steal a few cuys from the flock of the religious officer who, to our luck, lived about one hour from town and also had a house in town where he had a large flock of cuys in a big kitchen, as well as many chickens and rabbits.

We gathered in the town's plaza after dinner and proceeded to the religious officer's kitchen at the northernmost end of town. We caught eight cuys at random because we presumed that all cuys were ready for consumption (we were not interested in the chickens). Each of us had to take two cuys to the two girls' house. One detail we overlooked was that we forgot to bring a basket or a sack in which to carry the stolen cuys. Rusvel (for Roosevelt) and I hid our four cuys under our ponchos, while others put them under their clothes or wherever they could find to secure them. One of the boys was wearing a straw hat with a high crown; he hid one small cuy on his head and covered it with his hat. When he was crossing the plaza the cuy urinated on his head and, as he tried to wipe his hair, he dropped the cuy in the rose bushes in the middle of the park, and we never found it. The two girls' little brother, to whom we had served only a leg and the inner organs, reported us to the local school principal. The religious officer claimed that he was missing twelve cuys. All of our parents and guardians were summoned, the expectation being that they would replace the twelve cuys. It was our word against that of an honorable religious officer. The principal took us boys to his office, where he stood us in a line; he removed his heavy, thick belt, at which point we extended our arms for him to slash twice on each arm. Our grades on conduct dropped from excellent to poor, and our travesura became the joke in town until another mischievous action was discovered.

Changes in Cuy Raising

In Ecuador and Peru there are three models of raising cuys. These models are the household or traditional model, the community or cooperative model, and the commercial or entrepreneurial model. What MAG in Ecuador categorizes as small or family producers, middle producers, and large or industrial level producers falls into the third model of cuy raising.

Although the traditional method of raising cuys in the kitchen dates back many centuries, exploitation of the cuy using modern methods is a fairly new activity. Until recently, in any of the four Andean countries, neither scientific research for the purpose of breeding better specimens nor programs to promote raising cuys for local and national markets were seriously considered. Realizing that the highland areas present excellent and variable geographical conditions, national governments, nonprofit organizations, and private entrepreneurs have included the promotion of a more rational raising of the cuy at family or community levels because of the cuy's superior nutritional and economic potential. Cuy raising in Bolivia has still not changed from its traditional status. It will take at least another decade for researchers there to achieve what researchers in the other three Andean countries have accomplished, for the Bolivian breeders want to create their own indigenous cuy, independent of the Peruvian researchers from whom Colombia and Ecuador learned the new breeding methods.[11]

In 1967, scientists at the Universidad Agraria La Molina of Lima, Peru, realized that new generations of cuys were becoming smaller in size than previous generations, because people in the highlands were selling or consuming their bigger cuys and leaving the younger and smaller ones for reproduction. Researchers curbed this shrinking process of the cuy population by using a simple method. They collected cuy specimens from Arequipa,

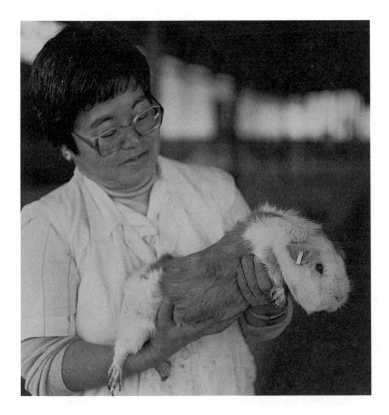

An agronomist of the Instituto Nacional de Investigación Agraria (INIA), Lima, Peru, holds one of her best specimens that weighs about 2 kilos.

Junín, Ancash, and Cajamarca departments where the traditional cuisine incorporates extensive use of cuys. They selected the best specimens for reproduction. By the early seventies researchers of La Molina had bred cuys that weighed as much as 1.700 kilos (Ayala-Loayza 1989:78).

Today in Peru, university researchers have bred the biggest, meatiest cuys found in the world. Before scientific breeding these animals averaged 0.75 kilograms, but those emerging from the breeding program weighed almost 2 kilograms.[12] When fed with balanced feed, a family could have available at least 5.5 kilos of meat per month without decreasing its flock (Chauca and Zaldívar 1989). If cuys are fed with forage only, offspring are not ready for consumption until fourteen weeks after birth, but if fed with balanced feed they can be slaughtered ten weeks after birth. INIA researchers recommend that, to obtain more meat faster, the basic, appropriate balanced feed must consist of corn, soybeans, corn-cobs, alfalfa, water, and one gram of ascorbic acid per each liter of water. When such feed is provided, the cuys consume from 22.61

Table 1.3 Increase in Weight Using Concentrated Feed

Feed (gr.)	Initial Weight	Final Weight	Increase
Alfalfa + concentrate	450.5 kg	825.5	378.0
Chinese grass + concentrate	457.9	821.5	363.6
Banana leaves + concentrate	453.0	787.6	345.6
Potato peels + concentrate	454.7	830.3	357.6

Source: Chauca (1989:21)

grams to 30.14 grams per day each with a resulting weight increase of from 7.17 grams to 10.21 grams per day (Chauca 1989:3). Alfalfa mixed with concentrated feed seems to be the ideal diet (see Table 1.3).

The INIA experimental station at La Molina in Lima plays an active and decisive role in breed improvement. Agronomists Marco Zaldívar and Lilia Chauca with a staff of three professionals have been devoted to the study of cuys for more than two decades. The experimental station has branch stations in many cities and towns throughout the country. The INIA, through its technicians, supports elementary schools, families, and small entrepreneurs by providing new breeds and technical assistance. The team of experts makes weekly visits to farmers, families, and schools that participate in the experiment. New breeds of cuys and scientific directions are provided to small household and semi-industrial producers.

The head of the INIA research office and her team visit families and farmers who raise cuys around the capital city of Lima to evaluate the participants' progress in the project. On a typical day the team surveys three to four families or production centers. I accompanied them on their rounds one day to get an idea of their work. The first stop we made was at an elementary school to which the INIA had provided two female cuys and one male. By June of 1990 this experimental educational program had well over twenty cuys. In this particular school, raising cuys is part of the curriculum, which consists of everything from planting corn in a small plot as a source of feed to learning the techniques of weaning, identifying the sex of the animals, learning characteristics of the different types of cuy, and cleaning the cubbyholes where the ani-

This family in Ecuador has taken advantage of the new method of raising cuys promoted by the Proyecto Palmira.

mals live. Since most people who live in this area are migrants from the highlands, the aim of the program is to introduce children to one aspect of their parents' culture. In addition to supplying the initial stock, the INIA provided the elementary school with material to build a room in which to keep the cuys. The agreement made was that the school would pay the INIA back in cuys rather than in cash as their enterprise grew. The school's Parent-Teacher Association (PTA) oversees all operations, and students are encouraged to start their own flocks of cuys at home. To protect animals from degenerating as the result of inbreeding, the researchers give producers "super males" bred at the experimental station in exchange for every male produced in the experimental program.

After visiting two families in the area, the team headed farther south where two farmers raise cuys at semi-industrial levels.

Leonardo Guardia migrated to Lima from the department of Ayacucho to establish his cuy farm, which he named after his hometown of Pausa, in an area where many other of his *paisanos* (fellow countrymen) have cattle ranches and pig sties. Guardia has over 1,000 cuys. Researchers claim that he resists scientific methods of raising cuys more than other farmers do. Despite the fact that scientific breeding has improved his business, Guardia still takes advice from the researchers reluctantly. Part of his experience in raising cuys includes using a mixture of cattle dung and cuy manure as fertilizer, which he claims to be the best. A few miles south of Guardia's place is the farm of Ismael Chauca. Unlike Guardia, Chauca is a native of Lima, and the cuy is not part of his culture. He follows religiously the directions from the researchers and has as many animals as his neighbor to the north. The day's fieldtrip ends with a late cuy stew lunch in a restaurant that buys cuys from Leonardo Guardia.

Marco Zaldívar, head of the research program in Peru, and Leonardo Guardia were murdered by the Shining Path in May and October 1991, respectively. Guardia's children abandoned their father's cuy production center because they were afraid of the possibility of more terrorist attacks.[13] Neither Zaldívar nor Guardia was involved in politics of any kind. The suspected motive for the killings was the guerrillas' anti-American feeling. The INIA had been awarded small grants by the U.S. Agency for International Development (AID) in Lima to aid people who were interested in being part of pilot programs. Zaldívar had been the recipient of a grant and Guardia was a target because he participated in the research program. Since Zaldívar's death, Lilia Chauca, his widow, has become an even more assertive and active researcher and is confident of the cuy's economic potential.

Today it is safe to say that many people, with the support from national universities and international nonprofit organizations, are raising cuy to satisfy the ever-increasing demand for meat. The INIA in Peru and the Ministerio de Agricultura y Ganadería (MAG) in Ecuador have divided raising of cuy for the market into three levels: small or family; middle or semi-industrial; and large or industrial. Small or family level producers are rural residents whose maximum number of reproductive mother cuys is 250 and who sell their cuys to maintain their business or make a small profit. Middle level producers are those whose number of reproductive mothers range from 250 to 500. Large or industrial level farmers are entrepreneurs whose flocks contain 1,000 or more reproductive mothers (MAG 1986). Ecuador, Peru, and Colombia have no statistics or estimates of the actual numbers in each of these categories of production. Middle- and industrial-level raising of cuy is concentrated mostly in the highland provinces of Imbabura, Pichincha, Cotopaxi, Tungurahua, Chimborazo, Azuay, and Loja in Ecuador. Raising of cuys is on the rise in Peru in the departments of Arequipa, Huancayo, Ancash, Cajamarca, Huánuco, and Lima. In Colombia, although most of the production is concentrated in the department of Nariño, entrepreneurs in the departments of Cauca and Valle are also raising cuys commercially. Commercial raising of cuys is gaining popularity in Ecuador, especially in areas where land conditions are ideal for the production of forage.

In urban populations few families raise cuys in the kitchen. In rural areas, families who live in one-room houses, or in areas where the temperatures are low, often share their room with their cuys, but they do not necessarily do so because of shortage of space; rather they live in the tradition of the older generations. A tapestry weaver in Salasaca in Tungurahua province, Ecuador, has a four-room house. The house consists of one bedroom, one kitchen, and one two-room working space where the weaver has his looms installed. In the kitchen, as well as in the bedroom, there is a wooden bedstead wide enough for six people. This family has about twenty-five cuys that are kept under one of the beds. When the feed waste and manure under the bedstead in the bedroom make up a thick layer of humid fertilizer, the cuys are removed to the kitchen. The cuy fertilizer is shoveled out into the yard to be dried and used in the corn plot or the orchard in the backyard. Although this has been the traditional way of raising cuys, the method is gradually being replaced by the newer, more rational methods.

In the highlands of Ecuador, the scientific approach to cuy farming is financed and supported by the Office of International Development of the Ministry of Foreign Relations of the Belgian government. An example of one of many projects being conducted in cooperation with the government of Ecuador is found in the province of Chimborazo. The Proyecto de Desarrollo Comunitario

An indication of the impact of the cuy economy on the quality of life is more visible in southern Colombia than anywhere else in the Andes. This woman resisted using the scientific method of raising cuys at first but went on to become president of the first association of cuyeras. She claims that the ten years she has dedicated to cuy farming has changed her standard of living dramatically.

In Chimborazo, Ecuador, women who participate in cuy economy have become aware of the need to find more sources of cash. Here, in a corner of a one-room school, adult women are taught Spanish and are trained in weaving.

Palmira operates out of the headquarters of a former hacienda (Totorillas), which during hacienda times was one of the largest private landholdings in the Chimborazo province. The goal of the
project is to work successfully with communities whose scarce
natural resources and lack of appropriate technologies hinder their
participation in the national economy in any other way. The project encourages and supports the rational exploitation of plants and
animals that are either native to the Andes or have been adapted
to the environment, such as quinua, potatoes, ocas, sheep, pigs,
and cuys.

The Palmira project is staffed by three Belgian experts and nine
Ecuadorian nationals of whom six are specialists in agriculture and
animal husbandry, two are drivers, and one is a live-in caretaker.
Of the six specialists, two are technicians and four outreach workers. In 1992, the technicians received a monthly salary of the
equivalent of U.S.$150 and the outreach workers, the equivalent
of U.S.$80. The operating budget for the project was about
U.S.$1000 per month. Salaries of the three Belgian technicians,
who are government employees assigned to the project, are depos-
ited in Belgium in dollars.

The project includes four communities of a total of approximately 600 families who inhabit 5,000 hectares of land. The goal
of the project is to change the traditional method of raising cuys
by first providing material to build cuy cages in space other than
the family's kitchen, and at no charge to the host families. Once
the *cuyero* (cuy cage) is ready, the project provides the family with
one scientifically bred male cuy for every ten female cuys in exchange for their traditionally raised males. Both the project's spe-
cialist in small mammals and the outreach worker assigned to the
community visit the cuyeros on a regularly scheduled basis. Rather
than lecture them, project members answer questions raised by
the peasants, for the whole philosophy of the project is to instill
in the peasants a sense of independence and to teach them techniques that will contribute to the bettering of their social conditions. The Palmira project's success is reflected in the fact that
people have not only increased their flocks by many dozens, but
they have also increased the quality of their cuys, that is, improved
protein to fat ratio.

In Tiocajas, one of the four communities that participates in the

Palmira project, by their own initiative a group of women representing about 100 families in the community decided to organize a *cuyera comunal* (a community cuy production center) to raise cuys. The Palmira project provided this group with materials to build a two-story brick building about 300 meters from the road that leads to Cuenca, the third largest city in Ecuador. This cuyera was officially opened on July 18, 1992, and practically everyone in the community of Tiocajas gathered to celebrate the event with music and drinks, roasted cuys and lamb. The cuyera comunal began its work with twenty female and two male cuys, which had been donated by the Palmira project. The project has committed continued support and technical advice until participating families learn the new methods of cuy raising.

The president of the Tiocajas cooperative (the woman at center holding the white sack) has organized families in the community to raise cuys. An outreach agronomist (the man at right wearing glasses) and the director of the project (the man without a hat next to the president), funded by the Belgian government, are also pictured.

The ground floor of the brick building that houses the Tiocajas cooperative project has been divided into eight one-square-meter brick boxes to hold about 100 cuys. The second-floor room of the community building serves as the living quarters for the family who acts as caretakers of the project's property. A different participating family moves into the center every two weeks to tend the cuys for the cooperative. And so the rotation continues. The scheduling of families to serve as keepers of the cuys helps fulfill another goal of the Palmira project: either to help people increase their caloric intake or to give them a way to earn cash that would otherwise be difficult to come by. Each and every family has the opportunity to gain more systematic experience in raising cuys, experience which they can then utilize in raising cuy flocks in their own homes. The consensus of the community seems to be that if the cooperative is successful, the next step will be to take advantage of the community's location by establishing an open kiosk where both the cooperative and independent farmers can bring their cuys to be roasted and sold to the local population as well as to tourists.

The Palmira was officially terminated on October 1, 1994. The three Belgian technicians left the country. Office and field equipment was moved to the Administerio de Agricultura's headquarters in Riobamba. The former house in the hacienda of Totorillas that served as the headquarters for the project is now practically abandoned. Given the lack of funding, distance of participating communities from Riobamba, and the ideological bias of the officials, it is unlikely that a national government will continue supporting programs for raising cuys that the Belgian government funded and implemented originally. However, the group of women of Tiocajas as well as many families in the area will continue to use the scientific methods of raising cuys because of the increase in demand for cuy meat and because it supplements the family income.

The attitude of people who make policy decisions in the Andes is that any effort of economic development to integrate the Indian or the peasant into the national life is hopeless. Because of the prejudiced position, government officials use the Indian cause to satisfy their own personal and group agendas. This attitude is more easily observed in the province of Chimborazo, Ecuador, where many non-Indian people are believed to be of pure Spanish blood (*sangre azul*), than anywhere else in the Andes. The political graffiti "Build your country; kill an Indian" (*Haga patria; mata un Indio*) that

I once read in the city of Riobamba epitomizes this middle-class mindset. The officials who fired the experienced technicians acted within this frame of thought. In light of the government officials' pessimism that the peasantry had potential for development, in the summer of 1994 the group of Belgian technicians who work in various projects were planning to propose that their government separate the joint Ecuadorian-Belgian projects, which were not joint projects in the true sense in the first place. Funds came from the Belgian government. The matching funds from the Ecuadorian government were minimal and consisted mostly in providing office space, inadequate though it was.

On my return visit to Tiocajas in the summer of 1994 I found that all families who had built their own *cuyeros* were producing cuys bigger than the ones they had produced prior to their participation in the Palmira project. By this time, no family had a single cuy left of their original lot. Despite two burglaries and the resulting loss of one hundred choice cuys in a single year (the equivalent of about U.S. $500), and even though project officials are not totally satisfied with the results demonstrated with this model of cuy raising, it has shown itself to be successful. In fact, it is so successful that during the dry season when forage was not available in the community, they were able to buy alfalfa feed with the

In the Andes it is rare to see men cooking, except for special events or on special occasions. Here members of the cuy cooperative of Tiocajas, Chimborazo, Ecuador, are roasting cuys and lamb to serve the community during the inauguration of the cooperative.

Members of the community came to the opening day of the cooperative of Tiocajas. Notice the smoke coming out from the first floor of the building where cuys and lambs are being roasted.

cash earned from the sale of their cuys. The material benefits from raising cuys have made families aware of the possibilities for bettering their economic status and caused them to reorganize their activities to ensure even greater profits. They have, therefore, refurbished the community kitchen in order to use it as a cuyera. Two women in the cooperative also went to Pasto, Colombia, to observe production and marketing of cuys so that they might further improve their own skills.

A second experience, this one in Colombia, illustrates the impact that cuy farming can have on regional economies and their social structure. In 1974 the Dutch and Colombian governments signed a contract whereby the Dutch government agreed to cooperate in an effort to stimulate dairy production in the Department of Nariño. In 1975 Dutch technicians realized that milk alone would not provide enough income to participating peasants so they changed their strategy. They decided instead on a project that would strengthen women's position in the community. They observed that women were the most involved family members in the raising of cuys. Even though the National Ministry of Agriculture was not interested in supporting the revised plan because cuys were not raised in other parts of the country and they had no model to look to, the Regional University and the Dutch proceeded to work together without national support. The Dutch and UNICEF each provided small loans to several groups of women. Peruvian technicians were invited to give short training courses, and scientifically bred cuy specimens from Peru were imported. When cuy production was shown to be a profitable enterprise, national banks began to offer small loans to individual women and, as would be expected in a male dominant society, men began to want to take over the marketing end of the business, leaving the women to do the work of running the farms. To prevent this from happening, women began to organize a cooperative called the Asociación de Productores de Cuy (Asocuy).[14]

In the summer of 1994, before visiting the women of Asocuy, I interviewed two technicians of Corporacion Fondo de Apoyo de Empresas Asociativas (CORFAS) who also have been promoting women's participation in cuy raising in the department of Nariño since the Dutch project was phased out in 1979. Later I double-checked information provided by the two technicians. In every case women asserted that their social and economic conditions had improved considerably after they started participating in what they called the "mujer-cuy" (woman-cuy) program. Each family had an average of 100 reproductive mothers that, in the best of conditions, could yield at least 400 animals per year.

Each of these three women earn as much as 100,000 pesos (U.S.$125) per month, 5 percent more than the national minimum wage. With their savings they have built a new kitchen, bought small household appliances, and paid loans obtained for agriculture to buy potato seeds and pesticides, or to buy work animals such as oxen and horses. Although the families who already have paid their bank loans off have established good credit records, they do not want to apply for new loans because the market for agricultural products such as potato, maize, and wheat is unstable. The cuy is the only product that has a stable market price.

Above and beyond the material gains from raising cuys, there is no question that the cuy is a catalyst for change in attitudes and behaviors within families concerning such things as the division of labor. Because of the profit women have shown in their cuy-raising enterprise, husbands no longer grumble as they once did about their wives wasting time in meaningless meetings. On the contrary they acknowledge and boast about their wives' new roles in the family and their position in society. Women are open and candid about their position to the point that some of them even claim to have reversed the traditional husband-wife relationship. One of the three women said in jest, "Now I am the one in the house who wears the boots." [15]

The Belgian technicians in Ecuador are trying to emulate this Colombian model of cuy farming. In Paquistancia, Pichincha,

An increasing number of families are adopting the scientific method of raising cuys. In a community in Pasto, Colombia, most families have cuyeros like the one pictured here, built with cinder blocks and located next to their houses. Each of these cuyeros can hold as many as two hundred and fifty animals.

three groups of women have organized themselves into three associations, the largest of which is the Asociación La Mano de Dios
with twenty-five members. Representative members of the three
groups of women filed applications with the Proyecto Agro-
Pastoril Cayambe, funded by the Belgian government to provide
them with initial capital, including cuy specimens. Once their pe-
tition was approved, the presidents of the three associations went
to Pasto, Colombia, to learn organizational skills from the women
there. The loans provided for the projects are paid off in installments. For instance, a loan of 900,000 sucres (U.S.$450 in 1993
sucres) is paid in nine installments. The first payment of 125,000
sucres (U.S.$62.50) is due six months after the loan is issued, and
the balance in eight installments of 98,000 sucres (U.S.$49) every
three months. The president of La Mano de Dios claims to sell at
least nine cuys every month at 12,000 sucres (U.S.$6) per cuy, in
addition to slaughtering a few for food. And she says, "Adoption
of the scientific method of cuy raising pays high dividends." It is
clear that few people, however, are taking seriously the cuy's economic potential. Throughout the Andes, few commercial operations report flocks greater than 2,000 cuys (Moncayo 1992c:1).

The biggest cuy production center in the world, which has set
the trend for the entire Andean subregion, is in Ecuador. Auquicuy,
which in the Ecuadorian Quechua dialect means "Prince Cuy," is
located in the Hacienda El Rosario near the small town of Salinas
in the province of Imbabura at 1,650 meters above sea level. The
temperature there ranges between 350°C and 160°C. The hacienda has a total of 20.5 hectares of land, of which 17 hectares are
planted with alfalfa, and 3.5 hectares with king grass. In 2,951
square meters (approximately one-third hectare) there are eight
cuyeros, and one 50-square-meter slaughter room. The cuy farm
employs appropriate technology to cut forage and to mix a balanced diet for the cuys. It also has ten full-time workers. Roberto
Moncayo, an agronomist who graduated from the University of El
Zamorano in Honduras, began the commercial exploitation of
cuys here in 1979 with 150 select females. In 1981 he introduced
scientifically bred cuys from Peru, and in 1983 he imported 273
more cuys from three departments in Peru. Since then Moncayo
has developed his own breed of cuy, the result of breeding the
Peruvian cuys with Ecuadorian criollo cuys. Currently, Auquicuy

View of the inside of one of the eight *galpones* (large cuy coops) of Auquicuy of Salinas, six miles north of the city of Ibarra, Imbabura, Ecuador. The coops hold more than 1,600 cuys each. Castrated male cuys run about on the floor and feed on leftovers that drop from the wire cages.

has 5,500 reproductive mothers and a total of 13,000 animals. Today, Moncayo's cuys are the ideal specimens for breeding to produce more meat in less time. People from all over Ecuador go to Auquicuy to buy at least a three-month-old male for about U.S.$10 (25,000 sucres). Moncayo's cuys are now known under the generic name of "cuys from Ibarra," after the capital city of the province of Imbabura near which Auquicuy is located.

In the Andes, people who identify themselves more with western culture associate cuy raising only with rural, rustic people's lifestyles, although many people in cities and towns raise cuys for their own consumption. The head librarian of the Ministry of Agriculture in Ecuador, in one of the many visits I paid to the library, told me the case of her cousin who had served in the Ecuadorian embassy in the United States and had decided to move back to Ecuador after many years of diplomatic service. Upon her arrival in Quito, she began exploring the possibility of buying land in the northern part of the country to open a cuy production center, for she thought that the market for cuy meat was promising. The librarian's reaction to her cousin's decision to go into such a business was totally negative. "How possibly could one think that a former diplomat would want to go into cuy raising?" she asked. "I could understand if she wanted to open a boutique or a first-class restaurant or a hotel, or seek a position in an important bank or international corporation. But cuy raising, my god, it is ridiculous," she concluded. The librarian thought that, as white as she looked, her cousin had some "Indian blood," and her decision to go into cuy raising was something like trying to find her identity, which she hoped was not the case.[16]

From Household Animal to Market Commodity

Escobar and Escobar (1976) demonstrate that the raising, consumption, and exchange of cuys play an important role in social order in the Andes. These activities connect the countryside with the city on the one hand, and people of different social strata and cultural backgrounds on the other. This is clearly observable in the open livestock marketplace in highland towns, as well as in large urban areas. In large cities such as La Paz, Bolivia, or Lima, Peru, small urban merchants, usually urban people, transport cuys from the farms to the market or supply animals to restaurants that include cuy as a specialty. To illustrate this I will describe some activities that take place in the cuy market.

Unlike the situation in Bolivia, Colombia, and Peru, live cuys are not sold in the mercados (buildings divided into booths to sell different products including live animals) of Ecuador. However, the cuy plays an important role in local economies. Cuy meat reaches asaderos (places that specialize in serving roasted cuy, rabbit, and chicken), modern and traditional restaurants, clubs, and family kitchens through three different avenues: open fairs, supermarkets, and direct producer-consumer transactions. Every town or city allows farmers from nearby areas to bring their products to be sold in the open fair. Municipal authorities have areas or streets reserved for this purpose (something like a farmers' market in the United States). In some cases, streets and plazas of towns or villages are practically taken over by these merchants, farmers, peddlers, and food vendors. These open fairs not only enliven remote populations but also support local businesses dominated by mesti-

The *mercado* of La Paz, Bolivia, where live chickens, ducks, rabbits, and cuys are sold every day. Notice that the two stands on the left carry more than one black cuy, which is a rarity in Peru and Ecuador.

zos and whites who take advantage of the occasion to sell or try to sell their manufactured products at inflated prices.

In the fairs and mercados of Latin America bargaining is a common practice. Traditionally, *casera(o)* was a Spanish term that denoted a special relationship between buyers and sellers, and it meant a "loyal" or "familiar" or "trustful" customer or merchant. The word described the nature of the relationship in which bargaining was carried out. Casera was also the very first word used by customers or prospective customers to describe themselves when they approached merchants. A casera always bought from the same merchant, who treated her differently from the other customers. A casera could buy merchandise on credit (*fiado*) or jump in front of the line to buy a scarce product such as sugar. A merchant might add for free a few extra grams of the product being purchased by the casera. Store owners attracted and kept customers by giving candies about the size of jelly beans to the children of caseras, and by giving greengrocers small bunches of herbs

In Cochabamba, Bolivia, this elderly woman is buying cuys from a household producer for a picanteria.

such as coriander. Today, the casera relationship in which the buyer-seller link was an intimate one is no longer practiced. Many years ago, both for buyers and sellers, the meaning of the word "casera" carried with it connotations of loyalty and even friendship. Today "casera" is a hollow word used by sellers of small animals, and by peddlers and other street sellers. However, bargaining (haggling over prices) is still very much a part of the culture.

In the marketplace, bargaining puts the peasant in an unequal position to the mestizo because of the given social, economic, and political conditions that prevail in Latin America, especially in the region of the Andes. Marking prices up and haggling over them are almost rituals and are practiced in the newly emerging cuy

In Huaraz, Peru, sellers, *rescatadores* (wholesale buyers and resellers), and housewives come to the marketplace early in the morning every Monday and Thursday.

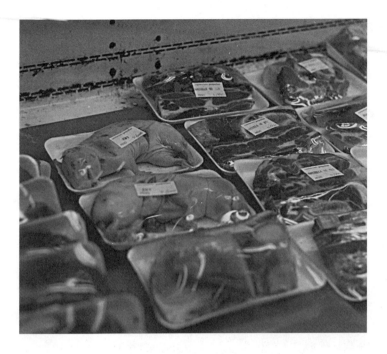

In Ecuador two well-known supermarkets carry prepackaged and eviscerated cuy meat. The price for one cuy is twice as much as one live cuy sold in the street market.

economy as well as the general marketplace. The amount of money that the peasant expects to obtain for his cuy (market value) depends on the prevailing prices at which cuys are sold (market price) and is subject to the economic laws of supply and demand as well as other factors. A peasant whose flock increases during the rainy season when feed is abundant may take his cuys to the weekly fairs organized by local governments, thus competing with other fellow peasants who are also enjoying a period of high production. Well-to-do farmers, on the other hand, who have the most productive land are able to capitalize on market conditions during the dry season when the number of peasants competing in the marketplace decreases because with no rain their production is down.

In addition to the bargaining advantage mestizos have, there are other aspects of marketing of cuys that make it difficult for peasants to compete. Transporting cuys to urban markets involves tedious and costly trips. Huaraz, Peru, is a city of about 50,000 people located about 375 kilometers northeast of Lima and is the capital of the Department of Ancash. Here, as in any modernized city, the local market has well-marked sections where wholesalers and retailers sell products from the immediate area as well as goods shipped in from other parts of the country. Every Monday

The *campo ferial* (fairground) of Guamote, Chimborazo, Ecuador, is well attended by peasants from surrounding communities.

and Thursday producers, wholesalers, and retailers from the countryside bring cuys in sacks, cardboard boxes, and crates, for which they are paid by weight. Prices for criollo cuys range from 2 soles (U.S.$1.20) to 3.50 soles (U.S.$2.05) depending on the size of the animal. Rescatadores (mostly women) buy up cuys from peasants at bus terminals or at the market and then sell them at retail prices to restaurants.

During the European invasion that began in 1492 the sovereigns of Spain sent chests of barter goods and merchandise to exchange or barter with natives for gold and other riches that they might have had. They called this type of transaction *rescatar* (Tyler

1988:118). Today in the Andes rescatar means to buy up goods from peasants who transport their products to cities and towns. In some communities rescatadores come to the outskirts of their town to buy up cuys at lower prices from peasants who, for one reason or another, avoid going into town. If producers themselves try to sell their cuys at retail prices, mestizos haggle over prices, and if they take their cuys directly to the restaurants, mestizos know they can pay them much less than they pay rescatadores. They do this because peasants are still barred de facto from modern facilities such as tourist restaurants. The cuy is a distinguishing factor between the countryside and the city, and class hierarchies remain in place, with the urban mestizo merchant controlling the social relations of production.

At the open fairs in such places as Guamote and Quero in the central highlands of Ecuador, the exchange between the urban and rural populations can be described as authentic. By that I mean that tourists have not influenced the dynamics of buying and selling in the ways they have in Riobamba, Otavalo, Pujilí, and Saquisilí

Some small mestizo producers bring their cuys to the fairs to sell. Bargaining is much more difficult when the seller is another mestizo.

In the Andes many women work harder than men. This woman in Riobamba, Ecuador, has walked for hours to bring her farm products to the fair.

where fairs are attractions staged for tourists. Women from communities that are as far as two or three hours walking distance come to the fair sometimes on mules and donkeys, but more often walking barefoot and carrying sacks of potatoes, vegetables, and cuys on their backs. Often their babies are tied on their chests. The more well-to-do peasants transport their sheep, cows, and pigs by truck, but by eight in the morning the *campo ferial* (a section of a community where live animals are sold) is already crowded with both buyers and sellers.

In the section reserved for the sale of small animals many sellers, mostly women, hold jute sacks or reed baskets with one hand, and a cuy in the other hand. Buyers from nearby urban areas bring with them an empty sack and many hundreds of thousands of sucres, depending on their need for cuys. The buyer approaches the seller by asking him or her to quote the price for the cuy he or she

Money from the sale of a cuy is often spent on fruits, candies, drinks, or spices. Oranges and bananas are being sold from the back of this truck, which has come from the coast to a fair in Guamote, Ecuador.

is holding. Prices range anywhere from U.S.$1 for a small criollo cuy to as high as U.S.$4 for a big cuy *mejorado* (cuy raised following scientific methods). Urban buyers offer prices as low as U.S.$.50 for criollo (indigenous) cuys and not any higher than U.S.$2.65 for mejorado cuys. Buyers always have the upper hand because they know that peasants need the cash to buy things such as salt, sugar, noodles, wax candles, basic medicinals, clothes, plastic shoes, or boots. After the bargaining is over, a three-month-old criollo cuy goes for about U.S.$1 and a mejorado cuy for about U.S.$3. The interesting thing is that some buyers resell the cuys they buy in the campo ferial in a different location in town, making a profit of about 25 percent for each cuy. Others resell them in other urban open fairs or supply asaderos with cuys.

Small experienced cuy farmers shop in the open markets for better male specimens. When they see big cuys these buyers usually try to bargain the price down, arguing that it is not for business. Some restaurant owners or those who earn a commission for their work also use this same argument, and many peasants are

This restaurant owner is buying cuys in the fair of Sangolqui, Pichincha, to roast in his restaurant in Quito, Ecuador.

already familiar with these business ploys. The mestizo farmer always attempts to outsmart the rural, rustic people and usually succeeds. Some urban or rural mestizos either make a living or supplement their income by supplying cuys to restaurants and asaderos. A team of two or three buyers goes to towns or villages on the day the open fairs are organized; they squat far from the section of the open fair where cuy producers and buyers congregate; one of them stays in the spot while the other two go to buy three or four cuys. Each member of the team can make about U.S.$3 in about three hours' work, in addition to the commission he or she gets from the restaurant or asadero.

In Ecuador, Bolivia, and Peru, the class conscious urban

mestizos and whites try their best not to come in direct contact with the rustic, simple, and illiterate country people. People who do not raise their own cuys in urban settings send their servants to buy cuys in rural fairs, or they buy ready-to-cook meat from people who cater to their needs. For middle-class and upper-middle-class people who buy their food from supermarkets pre-packaged, eviscerated cuy meat is readily available. Two well-known chain stores in Ecuador are Supermaxi and Comisariato Popular. The average price of .7 kilos of cuy meat at the Supermaxis, which are located in middle-class residential and commercial areas of Quito and Cuenca, is U.S.$4. Although prices are competitive, the amount of cuy meat sold at the Supermaxis is limited. Each store sells about fifteen to twenty cuys per day, and there are days when they do not stock the meat at all. Therefore, restaurants and asaderos rely on cuys available in open fairs or they buy them directly from commercial or industrial farmers.

Large industrial farmers are a permanent supply for regular, established customers. For instance, about 70 percent of Auquicuy's product is sold live from the farm site, while 30 percent of the production is slaughtered to fill orders from small restaurants around Quito. Seven restaurants, three in Carchi and four in Imbabura, get their year-round supply of cuy meat from Auquicuy. This farm's sale is approximately U.S.$7,300 per month, and the farm's major expenses amount to about U.S.$2,500 per month. On the average cuy meat is sold for U.S.$4.40 per kilo, and live cuys go for about U.S.$3.50 per kilo. This farm is so well known that people from as far away as southern Colombia travel up to six hours to buy cuys because demand in their own country is so much larger than the supply (see Table 1.4).

Unlike their counterparts in Bolivia, Ecuador, and Peru, cuy producers in Colombia have the upper hand in the buyer-seller arena. There is a shortage of supply by about 650,000 per year to satisfy the regional demand (Montenegro 1993:184), which is so high that buyers must pay higher prices to beat out the competition. Initially, producers transported their cuys to local markets. Today, restaurants and asaderos send their employees to visit producers on a regularly scheduled basis. These buyers bring cash with them to either buy cuys or to make advance purchases of cuys that will not be ready for a few weeks. No commercial producer

Table 1.4   Monthly Profit Analysis from Sale of 2000 Cuys
(in US$) in Auquicuy

Total production cost	$3,970
Sale of 1,896 kilos of meat	4,896
Sale of 12 metric tons of manure	266
Total sales	5,162
Net profit	1,192

Source: Statistics gathered in 1992 on the farm of Auquicuy near the city of Ibarra, Ecuador

takes her cuys to the marketplace anymore. Professionals at COR-
FAS did a careful market analysis and passed their findings to the
peasant producers. Producers learned the methods of merchants
who were accustomed to taking advantage of peasants and thus
avoided being underpaid.

The Best Organic Fertilizer

The cuy provides high quality meat, but that is not its only value
in the marketplace. Its manure can be transformed into a rich, organic fertilizer. Manure is always collected to fertilize gardens, or-
chards, and cornfields in the Andes. Some peasants use this high-
quality manure to fertilize coca plants in the rain forests. Small
farmers and wage laborers who raise their cuys usually improve
the quality of the coca leaves with cuy manure. For instance, 800
to 1,000 kilograms of manure can fertilize one hectare (2.47
acres) of land with 10,000 plants of coca (Rios-Reategui 1978:
6).[17] Many families who raise cuys value organic food and are concerned with the conservation of their cuy manure to produce their
own fertilizer. Three things are needed for the production of fertilizer: space, manure, and earthworms (Eisenia foetida). The procedure
is known as lombricultura. Depending on the amount of waste available, initial investment could range from U.S.$30 to U.S.$120.
Given the availability of waste, the major expense is the purchase
of red earthworms, known in South America as California earthworms or Red Hybrid earthworms. A one-hundred-pound sack of

red earthworms sells for the equivalent of U.S.$20. The rest of the investment is in boards and nails to build rectangular boxes on the ground. The process is simple and does not require extra labor, and it is a healthy and beneficial way of dumping cuy waste.

Rectangular boxes are placed on the ground at a slight angle so that water used to keep the boxes wet can drain properly; poor drainage kills earthworms. The sack of earthworms is spread inside the box first. Then, a thick layer of waste is added on top of the earthworms every time that cuy partitions or cubbyholes are cleaned, generally about every fifteen to twenty days. At an altitude of 2,500 m.a.s.l. it takes about six months to build up organic fertilizer in a box four cubic meters (8 x 1 x .50). One hundred pounds of this organic fertilizer sells for about U.S.$3. The waste of four hundred cuys is enough to produce about one metric ton of organic fertilizer every six months. The use of it in agriculture provides nutrients for plants for as long as two years and increases the ability of the soil to retain water. It is possible to grow organic forage that produces tastier cuy meat than that produced by commercial cuy farmers today using balanced feed.

Chapter Two

The Cuy as Food and
Symbolic Social Binder

In industrialized countries like the United States the cuy is humanized as a pet. It is given a name, treated almost as another member of the family, and taken to a veterinarian for regular health checkups. Its reproduction can be controlled and planned. But in its native homeland and in other places around the world where it is being introduced the cuy is raised mainly for food and goes through many phases of production, distribution, preparation, and consumption.[1] As a biological entity the cuy as food encodes implicit meanings. It is cooked using a variety of methods, is served on special occasions, and is ingested by commensals with varied table manners (Leach 1976:60). Types of food eaten and eating manners in any culture convey particular messages. Andean practices such as serving a shot of anisette after eating pork reveal the classification of foods as either hot or cold; or refusing to finish a three-course meal may mean disrespect for or rejection of the host. Food and eating manners convey even stronger messages when the meal, or the main course of a meal, is the best that a family or community can offer.[2]

Meals require the use of at least one utensil per head, a table, and a prescribed behavior. It is expected that solid food such as meat be cut or sliced with a knife and be placed in the mouth with a fork or at least with a toothpick. The acceptable ways of eating cuy, however, deviate from these particular sets of table manners. The size and shape of cuy meat lends itself to using both hands and fingers. In fact, using a fork and a knife to eat cuy may look awkward or out of place to people who are used to eating cuy with their hands. To many Andean people eating cuy is something like coming into contact with earth, fire, wind, and water that turned a living thing into a nutrient to maintain human life and growth. Food is a link between man and nature. Thus, *la vida* or *kawe* (life) often refers to an entity such as the cuy that embodies everything that man can experience through his senses, as well as things for which he has no explanation.

Many ideas and attitudes about food demonstrate people's understanding of life. For instance, people claim that food cooked in earthenware tastes better and is better for them than food cooked in tin or aluminumware. Another example is that in certain areas of the world people lick their fingers to show their satisfaction and pleasure and would not understand this action as being ill-mannered. But the cuy's place in the cuisine and eating behavior of Andeans is only a fraction of its overall role in Andean culture. As Leví-Strauss states, "The road from the wilderness to [man's] belly and consequently to his mind is very short, and for him the world is an indiscriminate background against which there stand out the useful, primarily the edible, species of animals and plants" (Leví-Strauss 1962:57). That is, besides being the best source of animal protein, the cuy has also many cultural uses and is a significant element in the Andean man's worldview, or what Luckman and Berger (1967) call social construction of reality or the formation of the Andean social being, which becomes part of an objective reality that is there to mold the individual independent of his will.

The rustic hearth in the kitchen with cuys huddling near it is a simpler life and more intimate than that lived in the modern world. In this simple world, for instance, the concept of the personal space within the family in interactions with others outside the family is nonexistent. Today in many highland communities that are undergoing modernization, children are socialized differently in families whose spatial arrangements are significantly different from the traditional distribution of space. These changes in the distribution of space parallel the changes in specialization and division of labor. Many activities such as harvesting quinua and collecting feed for household animals that were part of women's errands and children's chores are changing to adult male activities. The traditional grinding stone that was the only instrument available in the household to grind condiments and sauces to marinate meat has almost been replaced by manual or electric mixers and blenders. Aromatic herbs that were grown in the backyard are now available at *bodegas,* or supermarkets. Girls who were socialized to be good cooks and dedicated mothers follow instructions of elaborate recipes to make a good cuy stew. Storage and preservation of food that were hinged on techniques and technologies that were appropriate to varied climates and geographic conditions have yielded to household appliances.[3]

People's attitude toward food has changed tremendously during the last three decades. Before the seventies some people who, subjectively or objectively, claimed middle-class membership refused to eat sweet potatoes (*camotes*), beans, and roes. Having fried camotes for breakfast was an indication of poverty. Cuy meat was not common in metropolitan areas, except among immigrant people. Today, in Peru for example, the same social class that looked down on or ignored these foods would prefer having fried roes with rice or, in the best of cases, a cuy stew for lunch. As with sugar (Goody 1982:176), chili peppers, and chocolate (MaCamant 1992), changes in food attitude have motivated the shift in the production and consumption of food that not too long ago was connected to Andean lifestyle. As Goody concludes, "Cooking is closely related to production on the one hand and to class on the other. In a system of differentiated cuisine, often expressed and elaborated in culinary literature . . . [the] cultivation of taste also has its oppressive aspects" (Goody 1982:215).

Social class and social differentiation in food practices in the context of ethnic, social, and gender differences in the Andes has been documented by Weismantel (1988).[4] Because of the similar geographic, ethnic, and ideological characteristics that people throughout the Andes share, this work is valuable in understanding the connection between cuy raising and consumption, and social class. My interest here is to put the cuy in the context of what Weismantel has discussed about food in general. In the Inca Empire Andeans probably slaughtered cuys for the same reasons they do today, during religious ceremonies and special occasions (Reader 1988:169). However, even if this meant that the cuy was not a food exclusive to the elite, dominant groups may have had their own recipes and served the cuy in elaborate banquets to entertain regional chiefs and war heroes. More importantly, cooking of cuy was probably a marker of privileged labor among women who served the nobility.

Research presented in this book suggests that consumption of cuy meat is gaining acceptance among people who are not directly connected to the Andean culture and, eventually, it may regain its status as fine cuisine, such as it may have enjoyed during the Incas. It is probably safe to say that the current social and economic conditions in Latin America, especially in the four Andean countries, have driven urban people across-the-board to seek new sources of food. Today at least 275,000 cuys are slaughtered every day, and cuy meat is available at some supermarkets. However, although it is served daily at specialized restaurants, cuy meat is still a delicacy and is also susceptible to the subtleties of social differentiation.

Weismantel's conclusion that "food is one of the strongest of ethnic and class markers" (1988:9) is clearly perceptible in the consumption of cuy at family or micro and macro level. Irrespective of its traditional symbolism, the cuy as food is a sign of acknowledgment of power and prestige. Peasant families and communities entertain their compadres, political leaders, authorities, and foreign visitors with their best food. At the macro level the disparity between the simple countryside cuisine and the modern, urbane cuisine seems to mark class differences in the consumption of cuy. Dishes such as *fricase de cuy* (cuy fricassee) and cuy casserole sound more cachet than *cuy chactado* (fried cuy) or *cuy al horno* (roasted cuy). In a like manner proprieties of serving cuy are modified to conform to cooking and eating behaviors of people who are socially distanced from people with traditional folk ways.

Recipes published in newspapers, magazines, and cookbooks are designed to attract and intended to reach literate people. Literacy is an indicator of education, which, in turn, is the most viable means of class communication, at least in theory. Literate and educated people, who have a more sophisticated lifestyle and taste than the illiterate peasant, expect that food practices and table manners conform to their standards whatever they may be. Therefore, restaurants in middle-class sections of metropolitan areas that serve cuy dishes provide their customers with fingerbowls or toweletts to wipe their fingertips. This demonstrates that the use of the cuy as food is changing faster than other uses given to it such

In Arequipa, Peru, picanterías and restaurants feature the *cuy chactado*, which is similar to *cuy estirado* in Bolivia or *cuy frito* in Ecuador.

as in the traditional medicine, which still withstands the pressure from the outside world.

In Bolivia, Colombia, Ecuador, and Peru, well over 100 million cuys are slaughtered every year. As a pan-Andean delicacy the cuy dish binds individual or group reciprocities and social contracts, preserves cultural identities, and plays a part in various ceremonies and rituals. Archaeologists and anthropologists do not agree on the nutritional value of the cuy before the Incas. Rowe (cited in Bolton 1979:230) and Pozorski and Pozorski (1987:120) state that the supply of cuy meat during the Incas was important, whereas Bennett and Bird (1949:31) maintain that it was not as important. Nonetheless, given the prolific characteristic of the cuy and the degree to which agriculture was developed in the Andes, it may be true that the cuy along with the llama was responsible for providing populations with animal protein. Bolton (1979) maintains that consumption of cuys during religious festivities is an excuse for protein distribution. Others such as Archetti (1992) argue that the use of the cuy in rituals has very little to do with diet. It is only recently that the high protein content of cuy meat has gained popularity among nonpeasant groups, but among Andean people the cuy is still a special delicacy.

Table 2.1　Comparison of Cuy Meat to Other Meats

Species	% Protein	% Fat	% Minerals
Cuy	21.0	7.8	0.8
Poultry	18.3	9.3	1.0
Beef	17.5	21.8	1.0
Lamb	16.4	31.1	1.0
Pork	14.5	37.3	0.7

Sources: *Aliaga-Rodríguez (1989: 6) and the NRC (1991: 248)*

Table 2.2　Composition of the Cuy Carcass (%)

Part	Average	Female	Male
Muscles	58.82	59.24	63.30
Bones	13.54	20.19	14.00
Kidney	1.29	1.43	1.11
Kidney Fat	0.83	0.88	1.02
Head	18.48	17.05	18.13
Feet	2.14	2.27	2.43

Source: *Producción y Crianza del Cuy (Lima, Perú: Editorial Mercurio, 1987, p. 30)*

Transformation of meat to food is part of cultural creativity; for this reason recipes change from region to region. Above and beyond its nutritional value, meat, if subjected to scrutiny of hermeneutics, can reveal the totality of a human group; that is, social, structural, technological, religious, economic, and ecological characteristics of people converge in food and eating practices (Goody 1982:24). Cuy meat as food in the Andes is both symbol and sign (Weismantel 1988:8) that may be complemented with other substances such as alcohol to legitimize rituals and reciprocities (Mayer 1974). The process of transformation of the cuy as raw meat to food lends itself to the use of recipes as techniques that mark or characterize local or regional cuisines.

Both taste and nutritional value of cuy meat are far superior to beef, pork, lamb, and poultry (see Table 2.1). The quality and taste may change with the changes in variables, such as environment, feed, age of the cuy, and methods of slaughtering. People who have been eating cuy meat for many years claim that the cuy that has

been raised in the kitchen is tastier than the one that has been raised following scientific or commercial methods. In the dining room of a local hotel in Ecuador I met a young Cuban medical doctor who had been living in the country for almost two years. Whenever he wanted to eat cuy, this doctor would go to a small restaurant about two hours from Quito because the owner served only criollo cuys. He asserted that traditionally raised cuys tasted much better than cuys raised by commercial producers, and even better than the ones raised by his mother in the Province of Oriente, Cuba (see Table 2.2).

Slaughtering cuys is an occasion for women to socialize. The method used here is breaking the neck of the animal.

As seen in chapter 1, feed used and the age of the cuy are important variables in producing meat in quantity or of quality, whichever is the producer's priority. That is, cuy raising follows the same method that poultry, pork, and beef production do. Production of cuys for the amount of meat and for taste are mutually exclusive. It all depends on how quality of meat is measured and who the target consumer is. When a large amount of meat is required, such as in the case of restaurants and clubs that cater to large numbers of customers, quantity is more important than taste. Supply comes mostly from large producers. Conversely, when taste is more important than quantity the supplier par excellence is the small, traditional producer. Appreciation of cuy meat has to do with the concept that Andeans have about the taste of food, namely, sweetness that ranks higher in the food-taste scale (Archetti 1992:59).

The last variable that seems to be of significant consideration in the taste of meat is the method of slaughtering. The three most common methods of slaughtering are cutting the throat, breaking the neck, and asphyxia. Cutting the throat is the method used widely in Bolivia and in parts of Peru, while breaking the neck is used throughout Ecuador and in the department of Cuzco, Peru, and asphyxia is the method used in Colombia. When cutting the throat, the butcher grabs the cuy by its head, stands its hind legs on the floor, and cuts the animal's throat; then she holds the dead cuy head down to ease bleeding. When using the method of breaking the neck, the butcher holds the cuy in upright position, places the head in her right-hand palm and presses the head forward, causing a quick death. Asphyxia is accomplished by submerging the cuy's head in water for a few seconds. In the first and second methods blood is drained from the body through a small slit whereas in the third method blood remains in the system. Then the butcher dips the cuy in boiling water for a few seconds, peels the hair, and eviscerates it. People argue that breaking the neck is a more humane method of slaughtering, less painful for the cuy, and gives the meat a better taste.

Cuy Dishes

Generally, once it is seasoned and marinated for a few hours, cuy meat is broiled or roasted, boiled, fried, or a combination of boiled and fried. In broiling, the carcass is tied on one end of a stick and exposed to a charcoal fire. *Asaderos*, restaurants, *picanterias*, and *quintas* that specialize in serving cuy dishes broil cuys using semi-mechanized appliances that can hold as many as twelve cuys to be cooked at one time. To accelerate cooking and enhance appearance of the meat, oil or lard colored with achiote is applied as a glaze to the carcass with a brush or corn husk. The use of fat makes broiled cuy less appealing, especially to people who eat cuy meat because of its low-fat content. When asked about the fat that

In Ecuador, asaderos are often located near roads and highways so that truckers and commuters can have the convenience of stopping for lunch or dinner. Many people can afford only one-half or one-quarter of a cuy.

is used as the basic ingredient for a glaze, restaurants and street food peddlers usually claim that what they are adding is merely a seasoning ingredient. In Ecuador, although there are other methods of cooking, broiling and roasting are the most popular methods.

In Peru, recipes for cooking cuy meat are more varied than they are in Bolivia or Ecuador. In some areas, such as Cuzco, oven roasting is preferred over other kinds of preparation. Once a number of cuys have been slaughtered, the next step is to grind seasoning consisting of spices such as hot pepper, coriander, parsley, mint, onion, garlic, and salt, using a grinding stone or a small metal grinder. Then, the meat is seasoned and marinated from a few hours to overnight. Additionally, some people stuff cuys with fresh herbs, such as mint and oregano, to give the meat a special flavor. A brick or adobe oven is heated for about one hour if fueled with kerosene or for about two hours if fueled with wood. The carcasses are put in rows on flat tin sheets, then placed in the oven. An average brick or adobe oven can hold at least fifty cuys. Undoubtedly, roasting makes the tastiest and most nutritious cuy dish, and it is 100 percent natural. Roasting is the method recommended for cooking cuys that have been raised by commercial farmers who feed their flocks with manufactured, balanced feed, because it is a method that releases most of the fat. Families who do not have

their own ovens have their cuys roasted at bakeries or by neighbors. They are served with baked or boiled potatoes, parched corn, cheese, rice, and so forth. Broiled and roasted cuy is something like Chinese roasted duck in that it can be served with anything on the side.

Unlike the methods of cooking described above, frying cuy meat does not require any special appliances other than what already exist in the standard kitchen. My observations prove that there are two styles of frying cuy: *chactado* and *frito*, both of which are fried cuy with a slight variation in their preparation. At least one hour before frying, the cuy meat is seasoned with a sauce of garlic, onion, salt, pepper, and vinegar or cooking wine if available. Some restaurants cut the meat into five pieces, while others fry the whole cuy, then cut it in halves or quarters depending on

Many rustic picanterias have evolved into modernized traditional restaurants. El Chozon in Ibarra, Ecuador, now has a playground for children who come with their parents to eat at the restaurant.

During the celebrations of the Pentecost, this local baker in Ollantaytambo, Cuzco, Peru, roasted about three hundred cuys, for which he charged a small fee.

what customers prefer. At the household or family level, however, the cuy is almost always cut into five pieces. In the Department of Arequipa, Peru, people squash the meat with a slate on a flat grill. This is what is called *cuy chactado*. Both *chactado* and *frito* can be served with rice, boiled or baked potatoes, or salad.

In Ecuador, *sopa* or *locro de cuy* (cuy soup) is a common dish (Archetti 1992:69; Weismantel 1988:131). In Peru, any dish that entails boiling cuy meat is unheard of. In the Department of Cochabamba, Bolivia, however, *chanka de conejo* (boiled cuy) is a popular dish.[5] After soaking the meat in salt water for about two hours, it is cut into five pieces and boiled with beef bones, scallion, lima beans, potatoes, and mint. If customers want *conejo estirado* (squashed cuy), the whole cuy is boiled for a few minutes, placed on a flat surface, pressed with a slate, and then fried in oil or lard in a frying pan. In both *chanka de conejo* and *conejo estirado*, vegetables with which the meat is cooked are served on the side.[6]

A sixth type of cuy dish is known as *pachamanca*, also called *huatia*

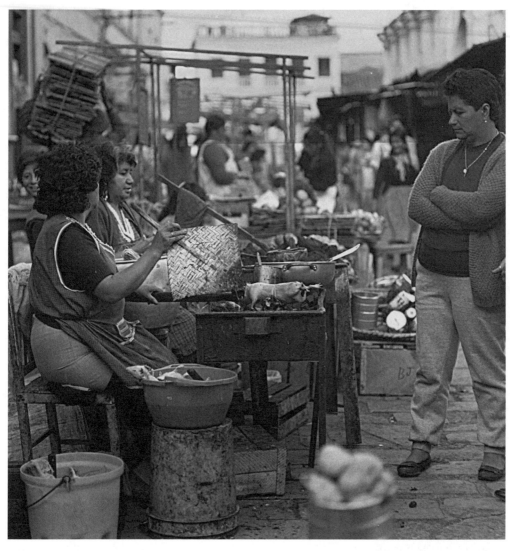

in some places. Literally translated, pachamanca in Quechua means "earthen pot." In practice it is a natural barbecue that, without any doubt, can be categorized as the best food in the Andean traditional cuisine. The things needed to cook pachamanca of cuy are firewood, stones, herbs, cuy meat, and vegetables. In the highlands of Peru doing pachamanca always requires group participation because of the amount of work involved. The group that organizes the pachamanca pools food and labor. Two or three people go early in the morning to build a small igloo-shaped oven with stones; another team brings boughs, shrubs, or wood for fuel. A

Many mestizos are uncomfortable with the slaughtering of cuys. They prefer to buy cuys where the meat is roasted while customers wait.

third group seasons the cuy meat (although lamb, pork, or venison can be substituted), grinds hot peppers, and provides pots, dishes, and silverware. It is the amount and the kind of meat cooked that determines the name of the pachamanca.

The oven is razed once it is red hot, and the *horneros* (oven builders) quickly place food on the stones. To help the food cook and to give it a special taste and keep the heat from escaping, workers cover the food with several layers of insulation. After the meat is seasoned with fresh aromatic herbs, two or three clean, empty woolen sacks or large paper bags are placed on top of it. Finally, a layer of dirt is shoveled on top to make a small mound. If any steam leaks out more dirt is shoveled on the mound. After about one hour, the layers of insulation are removed and the food picked up on trays, dishes, or corn husks. Ideally, pachamanca must be served along with *chicha* (corn beer), but, because this type of cooking is becoming more popular as a local, middle-class form of entertainment, beer, wine, and soft drinks are replacing chicha. Restaurants in urban populations roast meat and bake potatoes using adobe or brick ovens that are fueled with kerosene or timber, which they also call pachamanca.

In some places in Peru, local middle-class families cook cuy *pachamanca* on special events and occasions. The dirt that covers the pachamanca must be shoveled off quickly to avoid overcooking.

When done, cuys and other meat and the vegetables that have been seasoned with herbs and spices are removed quickly from layers of fresh aromatic herbs, clean woolen sacks, or large paper bags and dirt to avoid overcooking.

Cuy Dishes in Restaurants and Clubs

Up until recently cuy dishes were served only at a few restaurants in working-class neighborhoods in the Andes, and the supply of meat came exclusively from household producers. Scientific breeding has attracted more people to the occupation of raising cuys and has promoted mass production of the animals. Because of the ready supply of cuy meat and the increasing taste for it, some restaurants have begun including cuys on their menus, new restaurants that serve cuys exclusively have opened, and informal food stands have gained popularity.

Both in highland towns and cities and in large populations such as Cuzco many picanterias, quintas, and peñas (traditional restaurants) serve their cuy specialty. Picanterias and quintas cater to different kinds of customers. Picanterias are found in rustic environments and they serve chicha, which attracts peasants and the urban working class. Quintas are midway between modern restaurants and picanterias. They serve the same food picanterias do except that they do not serve chicha, and their customers are local middle-class people and tourists. Peñas, in their turn, are traditional restaurants in areas of large population, and they cater to migrants or people of highland ancestry who identify themselves with things Andean. Folkloric groups or bands that play music to entertain customers are either contracted or allowed to perform on the premises of peñas.

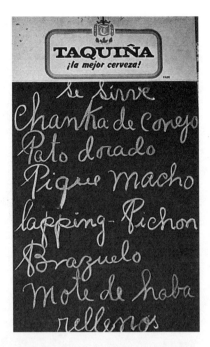

The menu of a traditional restaurant in Cochabamba, Bolivia, with *chanka de conejo* (cuy leg) on the top of the list.

For people not familiar with the use of the cuy as food, the sight of raw cuy meat is sometimes unpleasant.

In almost every city in Bolivia, Colombia, Peru, and Ecuador one finds traditional restaurants that either serve only cuy dishes or feature cuy dishes on their menus. For the sake of brevity here, I have selected cities such as Arequipa, Cajamarca, and Huaraz in Peru; Cochabamba in Bolivia; Ibarra in Ecuador; and Catambuco in Colombia where traditional restaurants serve cuy dishes daily or as their only specialty. Among the many that I have visited and

A typical cuy meal today is often served with beer rather than the traditional chicha. Beer is becoming more and more a popular drink.

observed during fieldwork, I can mention four restaurants: La Namorina of Cajamarca in northern Peru, La Chola Flora and Chota Flora of Cochabamba in Bolivia, El Chozón of Ibarra in Ecuador, and Catambuy in Colombia. When in 1978 I visited Cajamarca for the first time, the owner, a migrant from the small town of Namora, had opened a picanteria in a shack built with reed mats and tin sheets on the south side of the road that leads to the thermal baths of the Incas. Today La Namorina is the most famous picanteria in the city. National and international tourists visit to savor its fried cuy served with stewed potatoes or rice or unhusked, boiled wheat (*trigo pelado*).

In Cuzco, Peru, roasted cuy is the main ingredient of the *chiri uchu*, which is a traditional dish something like turkey at Thanksgiving in the United States.

La Namorina is so successful that other picanterias remain marginal and cannot compete with it. In the summer of 1990, due to their frustration in not attracting as many customers as La Namorina, the owners of two restaurants in the area spread the rumor that La Namorina was serving rat meat instead of cuy meat. This rumor scared away a few local customers, but foreign and national visitors who make up the bulk of La Namorina's customers did not know of the rumor, and others from the area knew how to recognize cuys and ignored it. This rumor is totally unfounded because rats are not as big as cuys, nor do they have as much meat on them as cuys do. Cuys of Cajamarca are among the best in Peru because the scientific breeding promoted by INIA has had an effect on cuy raising there, and irrigated lands produce good quality forage, especially alfalfa.

In Cochabamba, Bolivia, two traditional restaurants are well known for their *cuy estirado* and *chanka de cuy*. These two restaurants are both located in the same section of the city and cater to their own clientele. Coincidentally, the owners of these restaurants are both named Flora. To differentiate one from the other, people have nicknamed each woman using socially identifying terms that are widely used in Bolivia: *chola* and *chota*. Chola is a social category that describes a woman whose traditional dress coincides with her native physical appearance. Chota is a term used to label an Indian woman in western dress. Chola Flora is open from Thursday through Sunday and Chota Flora seven days a week. Chola Flora operates out of a modern brick and cement building, and on weekends reservations are required, whereas Chota Flora's is conveniently open from ten in the morning to six in the evening. The owner keeps at least six cuys in a wire cage ready to be slaughtered to serve to customers. Chola Flora has her staff slaughter cuys early in the morning and cooks them as customers order either chanka or cuy estirado.

In the province of Imbabura, about three miles south of the city of Ibarra, is the small population of Chaltura where the traditional restaurant, El Chozón, serves only cuys and fried chicken. Here the price for a whole crisp, fried cuy served with boiled potatoes, salad, parched corn, and hot peppers on the side is 14,000 sucres (U.S.$7). El Chozón gets its supply of cuys from small producers in the area and from Auquicuy, an industrial cuy production center about fifteen miles north of Ibarra, and pays an average price of 10,000 sucres (U.S.$5) per each cuy. El Chozón's profit resides in the number of fried cuys served. This restaurant is open seven days a week and can serve as many as 400 cuys per week. The original leaf-thatched building had the capacity to seat only about twenty-five people. Most of the time customers could expect to wait for an hour to be seated. Both the restaurant's popularity and the increasing taste for the cuy have created the need for a bigger and more modern salon. A salon with the capacity to seat about 250 customers that features a small playground for children was opened in December 1993. Other cities, such as Ambato and Cuenca, have sections where cuy asaderos also serve a limited number of roasted cuys at much higher prices than El Chozón. For instance, in Ficoa, Ambato, a whole roasted cuy that weighs about 0.800 kilos sells for 25,000 sucres (U.S.$12.50).

On the outskirts of the city of Pasto, Nariño, Colombia, are eighteen asaderos (Montenegro 1993:182), and five of these asa-

In Ambato, Ecuador, restaurants that serve broiled cuys every day have devised a manual revolving broiler that takes as many as six cuys at a time. Here a whole broiled cuy sells for about U.S.$9.

deros are in the township of Catambuco. The oldest, most well known of these asaderos is Catambuy, built on 4,480 square meters of land. This asadero has four salons that can seat a combined total of 300 customers; it has a discoteque and a parking lot for twenty cars, which attracts people who otherwise would not go to asaderos. It has eight full-time employees and ten part-timers who are called upon when their services are needed. The founder, Arnaldo Peñafiel, went to Peru to learn modern cuy-raising techniques, and in 1972 he built this asadero. Catambuy is open seven days a week throughout the year, except on Good Friday. The current manager claims that all the cuys served come either from his family's farm or from local producers, and that they do not serve cuys fed with food concentrate. I found Catambuy's roasted cuy, however, to be too fatty and to have a slightly fishy taste and mealy texture. It left a taste in my mouth and on my fingertips not characteristic of cuys that have been fed only with forage.

Because of their increasing popularity, cuy dishes are also sold increasingly in informal settings. Women sell roasted or grilled cuys from stands and wheelbarrows at the marketplaces or along busy roads. In the Mercado Nueve de Octubre of Cuenca, Ecuador, roasted cuy vendors set their barrows up at about 5 o'clock in the afternoon when vegetable, grocery, and fruit vendors and street peddlers have cleared the area. Each and every woman brings

about twelve seasoned cuys, charcoal, and a charcoal stove. Roasting is done one cuy at a time. Preparers tie the cuy on a stick and hold it over the charcoal fire. Lard or oil is used as a glaze to accelerate cooking. Some customers take the roasted cuys home wrapped in plastic bags; others bring their own plastic ware for carrying out roasted cuy, while some customers buy the raw, seasoned meat to cook at home. The price for a whole roasted cuy ranges from 8,000 to 12,000 sucres (U.S.$4 to U.S.$6) and a few cents less per cuy for uncooked meat.

In Mocha, a village about 150 kilometers south of Quito, on the east side of the Pan American road, I found a rest area where trucks, buses, and cars transporting tourists stop for a snack or lunch. In this rest area three food vendors sell potatoes stewed in peanut sauce, coffee, banana chips, soft drinks, and roasted cuys. Each of these vendors sells at least fifteen cuys on any given day at an average price of 9,000 sucres (U.S.$4.50) per criollo cuy. Since Mocha is located at an altitude of about 2,800 meters above sea level, the temperature in the winter is not any higher than 15°C. To keep the food warm, vendors cover their pots with a thick layer of brown paper and many layers of heavy woolen blankets. These vendors buy their supply of cuys at the open markets in Riobamba, Quero, and Ambato on Saturdays, Sundays, and Mondays, respectively. Because of the strategic location of Mocha, the village is well known for its cuys. National and foreign tourists stop there to taste the cuy. Oftentimes, the three vendors run out of roasted cuys in a few short minutes. I saw this happen myself one day when a busload of French tourists stopped at this rest area and exhausted the three vendors' supply of cuys in ten minutes.

In Peru, the leading country in cuy raising and the center of the Andean culture, cuy meat has gone one step beyond its traditional, ritualistic use. Consumption of cuy meat is no longer confined to the kitchens of regional clubs and restaurants that serve ethnic foods. It has made the glass display cases of expensive restaurants in exclusive neighborhoods and attracted the interest of creative entrepreneurs. La Tranquera is a grillroom located in the middle-class district of Miraflores in Lima, Peru, and it is always crowded. When customers drive up in the front of the grill room, a parking attendant takes the customers' keys and escorts the party to the lounge. A waiter greets them, hands them the menu, and offers them a complimentary drink of their preference. Another waiter escorts them to the table and takes the order for appetizers and drinks or refreshments—a typical kind of scenario in an American restaurant of high quality. A few minutes later, the same waiter invites and encourages the customers to make their choice of an entrée at the glass case in which meats are displayed. A grilled cuy of about 800 grams goes for the equivalent of U.S. $15. Obviously, La Tranquera's customers are tourists and upper- and middle-class nationals who may or may not come from Andean ancestry.

In the Valley of Huaylas (nicknamed "The Peruvian Switzerland"), famous for its snow-capped mountains that boast the second highest peak in South America, *picante de cuy* is a popular regional dish. Although *pachamanca de cuy* is served at the *recreos* (local name for traditional restaurants), oven roasted or grilled cuy was almost unheard of in the area until 1992. That year on the main street of Huaraz an entrepreneur opened a restaurant whose specialty is broiled cuy.[7] By local standards, the Cuy Broaster is an elegant setting furnished with wooden tables and chairs and is open for lunch and dinner. Its customers are mostly European tourists. (The flow of American tourists has dropped dramatically

A mestizo, middle-class, fund-raising activity is an opportunity to eat *picante de cuy*. This party was organized by the Club Departamental Ancash in Lima, Peru, to honor sixteen outstanding teachers.

because of terrorism that Peru has been experiencing since 1980.) Only a few locals can afford to pay 3 soles (U.S.$1.20) for a quarter of a cuy. The owner gets his supply of cuys directly from small producers in the valley and occasionally from resellers on Mondays and Thursdays when the local food fair takes place. For people who are not familiar with Peruvian and regional cuisine and for people who try to avoid contracting diseases such as cholera, broiled cuy is a safe brown bag lunch or dinner to take along to the field, on a sightseeing trip, or to the office.

To eat cuy meat requires an etiquette distinctive to the task, as well as the ability to nibble every bit of it. One can tell by the size of the heap of bones in the plate who is good at eating cuy meat and who is not. Regardless of the mastery of the etiquette, the tufo (strong, denouncing smell), a somewhat sweet smell stays on the hands and fingertips for as long as twenty-four hours after eating the cuy, even if one washes with soap. The trick to getting rid of the smell is to dip the fingers and wash the hands with beer. It is fascinating to observe how some people appear conscious of the need to get rid of the smell, especially upper-middle-class people, while others find creative ways of dealing with the tufo.

During my stay in southern Colombia in the summer of 1994, a group of graduate students and faculty of the Universidad Nariño took me out for a cuy dinner in Catambuy. The waiter served us toasted maize and popcorn as appetizers; we each ordered one cuy and one twelve-ounce bottle of locally distilled rum to go with the cuy (*para asentar el cuy*). The manager, who also is faculty in another local university, made sure that the cook roasted what seemed to be the cuys he stocked in the den. Toward the end of dinner I noticed that each of my hosts put aside about one fourth of their cuys to take home. Metaphorically, this portion is known as *parar-rayos* (lightning rod), which stops any argument or complaint from the spouse or girlfriend who was waiting for dinner at home. The characteristic tufo leaves no room for excuses, explanations, or lies.

A Symbolic Social Binder

Under many regional names, a cuy meal is a delicacy reserved for special social events. As a ceremonial food cuy is offered when opening formal negotiations of one kind or another. The occasion might be a traditional marriage or a time set aside ahead to ask for a favor or to request that someone be a ritual kin such as padrino (godfather). Cuy might be served also to honor a special guest or political figure. Locally, when an infant is christened or when a boy gets his *quitañaque* (first haircut), parents host a dinner for their child's godparent(s) and guests, which includes chicha and the best meal possible. The cuy dish is always the main course. In exchange for the special treat, the godparents respond with presents for the child that, depending on their economic status, may range from domestic animals to a patch of land.

The cuy is also used as the main component of a ceremonial treat known as *shimi kichay* (mouth opener) that invariably includes coca, chicha, or alcohol. When the recipient of the *shimi kichay* is a single male or the offering family does not know of the recipient's food practices, the shimi kichay is handed over *chawa* or *chawampa* (uncooked or live). In the *sirvinacuy* (common-law marriage), after the parents of the would-be couple reach an agreement, or as a preamble to the negotiations to unite their children in matrimony, the groom's parents offer the bride's parents a cuy stew. Acceptance of this food by the bride's parents or guardians is a sign of allowing initial conversations about marriage, or at least courtship negotiations, to begin. Following the traditional meal, many rounds of alcoholic drinks are served, along with coca for chewing. The bride leaves her home to form her own family or to become part of her husband's family, or in some communities the new couple may stay in the bride's family's house or migrate to an urban setting.

Oftentimes, mistakes or mix-ups result when the shimi kichay ritual involves wealth and a lot is at stake. Chicha and *trago* (a generic term used for alcohol) are plentiful on these occasions. I collected one story about Pedro Rios, who had worked in Lima for five years before returning to his village and deciding to settle down. A few weeks after his arrival Pedro asked his mother to approach the parents of the woman whom he had chosen to be his wife. Pedro's mother asked her older brother to act as the head of the family in the negotiations with the parents of the proposed wife. The woman Pedro wanted to marry was the eldest of four daughters. Pedro's mother cooked two *jaca pichu* (stewed potatoes and fried cuy) using four cuys and brewed chicha, and she bought three bottles of alcohol and a few ounces of coca. One Friday evening Pedro, his mother and uncle, some friends, and I got together and started drinking alcohol as if we were warming up for a long night. Pedro's mother brought in the two jaca pichus, the uncle the bottles of alcohol and coca in a saddle bag, and a neighbor an arybalo with many gallons of chicha. I brought with me my tape recorder and cassettes of huayno music. Pedro asked me

At this wedding reception in Salasaca, Ecuador, segregation by class is accepted and institutionalized, as it is in many communities in the Andes. Friends, neighbors, and relatives of the newlyweds are gathered in the yard to celebrate.

to play a song whose lyric in Quechua went something like, "Let me go, let me go because if your mother finds me red-handed she will think I am her son-in-law." When we entered the house of Pedro's proposed in-laws the family was sitting in the yard. The four young women rushed out to the cornfield in front of the house and from there they each sneaked into their room one by one.

Pedro's uncle served the father of the wife-to-be a shot of alcohol, and the party began. Upon finishing one bottle of alcohol Pedro's uncle and the parents of the girl went into the kitchen where they stayed for about one hour. The girls remained in their room, and Pedro and company sat on adobe bunks attached to the

Mestizo wedding guests are seated inside in the living room where fried pork (*fritada*) or cuy, champagne, and soft drinks are served.

wall. After the negotiators had reached an agreement, the wife came out of the kitchen and went into the room where the four girls were waiting to see which of them would be leaving the family that night. A few minutes later the mother took her eldest daughter, Susana, who was sobbing, by the hands into the kitchen. Pedro was summoned so that he could receive his father-in-law's blessing as a new family member. According to the dictates of the community's tradition, the union would be consummated in the new husband's house. Pedro's new father-in-law requested that we continue to party, for there was plenty to drink but not much to eat other than parched sweet maize. He also requested his first-born child to "become a woman in his house."

It was the mother's responsibility to have her newlywed daughter sleep in a separate room to give the couple privacy. Pedro's understanding, as well as that of the group, was that Susana would stay in the room where she usually slept with her three sisters, and the sisters would move into the room upstairs or into the kitchen. The mother failed to separate Susana because she got drunk after two drinks of alcohol. The party went on well past midnight; most of the group including Pedro could hardly walk, and Susana's parents passed out. Pedro asked his mother-in-law, who could hardly utter a word, where Susana was. I heard her saying, "In the big room." Pedro went to the room indicated where his wife awaited him, and he slipped into the middle of the bed on the floor where Susana and her three sisters were sleeping. He spent the night with the youngest of the four girls, and Susana assumed that her parents had decided to "give their youngest daughter away." The mother, somewhat sober now, got up to cook diced potato soup with hot red peppers. We all, except Pedro, realized the mix-up.

Pedro was sleeping soundly with a thirteen-year-old girl sobbing beside him. The father woke Pedro up to scold him for his behavior. Pedro responded by blaming his mother-in-law. Three different propositions arose to solve the problem. The mother wanted Pedro to accept Isabel as his wife; the father declared the ritual invalid; Pedro and his family contested that they had come with their jaca pichu for Susana. In an altercation, siding with her husband, Susana's mother said in Quechua to Pedro's mother, "Take your male hog home and let's get this nonsense over with." Pedro's mother responded by saying, "How dare you call this nonsense after you have accepted my jaca pichu and got drunk on my alcohol." In the end, Pedro won the case, and we went back home with Susana. I jokingly suggested having another party. The father emphatically reacted, saying, "No. Please leave before another mix-up happens."

On occasion, parents may find themselves in embarrassing situations after accepting ritual food if their daughters defy their decision to "give them away." This is sometimes the case, especially if children have been exposed to a culture in which marriage practices are different from the ones with which they have grown up, or if children have already experienced romantic love.

Francisca, a twenty-year-old, tall and physically mature young woman from a small village, fell in love with a man who had come to the community as a substitute teacher for one academic year. When the teacher left the village, Francisca followed him because she was pregnant, only to find out that the teacher was married to another woman. After almost a year she and her first-born child came back to her village. Ananias, a boy who had been attracted to Francisca even when he knew she was in love with the teacher, told his parents of his decision to make Francisca his wife. Over drinks of alcohol in a nearby town Francisca's father agreed to celebrate the traditional wedding.

On a date that the two fathers secretly set, the boy's family showed up with food and drinks at Francisca's house. Again, as described in the above case, after following the proper etiquette for the ritual, the parents informed Francisca of their decision. To everyone's surprise the girl refused to accept the fate that her parents had decided for her. She screamed, yelled, and scolded her mother, saying in Quechua, "You ate the cuy. I did not. Now, you open your legs to him, not me." Despite her defiance, Francisca was forced to take Ananias as her traditional husband. The mother held Francisca's baby, and the father physically dragged her to a room where she would spend the night with Ananias, now her husband. It was clear that the parents were forcing Francisca into this because she had disobeyed them when she left home to follow the teacher whom she loved. The defiant girl was humiliated, but in the end, she prevailed because the traditional wedding was not consummated. Instead, when, on the following morning, the parents unlocked the room, they found Francisca sitting by the door and Ananias lying on the bed showing scratches and bruises all over his face. Francisca had literally knocked him out. As she came out of the room, she reiterated her remarks about the cuy dish and fled to the nearest town where she was employed as a housekeeper and became the lover of a local policeman.

These two cases of arranged marriage clearly illustrate the extent to which the cuy as a ceremonial food is used to mark the transition or passage from one status of life to another. This ritual is known in Quechua as *ashinakuy*, which literally means to seek after each other, but in practice means to seek for a bride. When, in some cases, the arranged marriage is intended to end a romance of two people who may have kept their love secret, it is known as *casaratsiy* (wedding arranged without the couple's knowledge or consent), a formal legal religious or civil ceremony. Only in a few cases is ashinakuy kept from public knowledge, like in the case of Francisca. The suiting family's activities prior to the arranged marriage ritual usually become the gossip in the neighborhood or the community. Activities that make the preparations for the ritual conspicuous may include borrowing a cuy, seeking the services of an expert matchmaker, brewing small quantities of chicha, or buy-ing alcohol and so forth.

What is important in the two cases described above for the pur-poses of this book is not so much the rites of passage as social and psychological processes, but rather how the jaca pichu is used symbolically to mark the communion of individuals, families, and communities. As such, the jaca pichu's role in the ashinakuy is to make public what is private, or social what is personal.

The cuy also plays an important formal role in helping highland migrants who are settling in metropolitan areas come in contact with other newcomers or with children of earlier migrants. A *cuy-ada* (generally lunch featuring cuy as the main course) is an occa-sion for people to gather from a highland town to celebrate their patron saint's day away from their native land, or an event to raise funds to benefit a community cause or to honor an outstanding paisano. A cuyada can take place during street fairs, social club activities established in urban areas by highland migrants, and during sports competitions and important holidays. People volun-teer to bring to these events a *vianda* (a tray containing ready-to-serve food), something like a potluck in America, except that it is sold rather than shared with other people.

Cuy in some form is also served at every nonprofit fund-raising lunch or for-profit street fair. On June 6, 1991, a social club made up of residents of Ancash in Lima, an organization that is domi-nated by civil servants, business people, and middle-class profes-sionals, organized a fund-raising lunch. At the same time, the lunch honored sixteen distinguished teachers from the sixteen provinces of the Department of Ancash. The menu included corn tamales as appetizers and *picante de cuy* Huaraz style as an entrée. The price of the tickets was the equivalent of U.S. $8 per person, and the tickets were sold out after a few minutes.

The variety of foods that Spaniards brought to the New World changed the diet and cuisine of both Americans and Europeans. In America, the dominant conquerors stigmatized indigenous be-haviors and denigrated consumption of "Indian" foods. In many ways the negative attitude toward "Indian" food that Latin Ameri-cans inherited from their Spanish conquerors has not changed and is evident today in Andean society; to a great extent, the

consumption of cuy meat is another layer of ethnic and class markers (Weismantel 1988:9). While the peasant cuy dish is a ritual
food for many, it is for others a display of social class. To Andeans,
a social or religious event in which cuy is plentiful is talked about
for many months. Families who raise cuys for cash stop selling
them long enough to save enough animals to celebrate the special
occasion. Sometimes that might be as many as fifty animals. Those
who do not raise cuys get personal loans to buy cuys, which are
paid back in installments over as long a time as two years. I have
observed this to be more the case in Colombia than in the rest of
the Andes. It is a display of social class in that a lunch consisting
of one cuy and drinks for a family of four people costs about
U.S.$40, that is, the equivalent of approximately 30 percent of a
minimum monthly wage in Colombia, and about 65 percent of
the monthly wage in Bolivia, Ecuador, and Peru.

Chapter Three

The Cuy in
Andean Medicine

In most parts of the Andes, medicine as it is practiced in the United States is either nonexistent or culturally rejected. If the traditional medicine that is available in the household proves ineffective in a given treatment, a patient is almost always taken to a folk doctor in the community. The folk doctor's method of healing and the patient's physical condition both determine whether the cuy is used to diagnose or cure the patient. Before diagnosing a patient's illness, the folk doctor often chews coca and drinks chicha, or alcohol, to prevent diagnostic mistakes. The patient, or the patient's family, provides coca and chicha or alcohol. The folk doctor rubs the patient's body from head to toe with a live cuy (some *curanderos* prefer black cuys).[1] Then he slits the animal's abdomen, examines the rodent's organs and either diagnoses the illness or pronounces the patient's cure.

Curanderismo, an Andean healing practice, and the shops that stock supplies needed in the healing sessions are found almost everywhere in Latin America, especially in areas that have sizable numbers of people who have Andean roots. When Lourdes Soto of Lima suspected that her husband was having an affair with another woman, she did not seek professional counseling or resort to praying to the saints that she be found preferable to the other woman. Nor did she try to confront her husband with the changes in his behavior. Instead she went to a *curandera* to have cards read for her. Likewise, after serving time in a state prison for drug dealing, José Ramos decided to go back on the streets of Spanish Harlem, New York, to get new suppliers, but he first visited the nearest *botánica*

to buy customized candles adorned with herbs, oils, incense, and prayers written on parchment paper. Some people may think that Latin American immigrants turn to the supernatural for solutions to their problems because they cannot afford professional help, or that they do not trust other physical and spiritual methods of healing. Others would argue that seeking supernatural solutions for biological and social problems is a matter of faith. Actually, the supernatural in most parts of Latin America has always been directly bound to nature in its different forms and states. In the Andes, the coca leaf and cuy, along with other herbs and animals, bind man to supernatural powers.

In the traditional Andean health system, ill health is considered to be disequilibrium that is attributed to several causes: food classified as *frio* or *caliente* (cold or hot), *wayra* or *mal aire* (draft), *susto* (fright), *brujería* (witchery), and spells cast by spirits of ancestors and earth, and by God. Depending on their specialty and location, people who practice medicine following their own method of healing and using resources available in nature are known as *curanderos* (folk doctors), *brujos*, *parteras* (midwives), *herbalistas* (herbalists), *entendidos* or *curiosos* (those who understand or are skilled), *altomisayocs*, *yachaqs*, or *llatiris* (sages), *pusangeros*, *ayahuasqueros*, *hueseros*, and so forth. In many communities in the countryside as well as in urban areas, at least 25 percent of people in the Andes resort to traditional methods of healing (Barahona 1982:141).

In the Andes scientific medicine is delivered through official state institutions and private profit and nonprofit institutions such as hospitals and medical posts, which are available to urban populations and, theoretically, accessible to rural populations. Recently, scientifically based health practices have been extended to many remote populations and communities, even have been imposed on native people without any holistic evaluation of the culture. In other words, neither health professionals nor policymakers understand the culture with which they are dealing. Traditional medicine is connected to rituals, metaphors, and symbols familiar to the Andean people. Therefore, incorporation of modern, scientific methods of diagnosis, prognosis, and treatment of illnesses leads to confrontation with practices that have deep cultural roots. In many communities where health professionals refuse to live, curanderos are the hope for the indigenous people (Bastien 1987:5 and 1982:163); and places such as Iluman in Ecuador, Salas in Peru, and Kollawaya in Bolivia still attract dozens of people of different social backgrounds.

Jaca shoqpi (rubbing with cuy) or *soba con cuy* and *cuypichay* (to clean with cuy) are practices often referred to as "the Andean X-ray." They have popular appeal throughout the Andes. In many areas in the highlands as well as in coastal cities, the jaca shoqpi is a very popular method of healing, and those who perform it observe a defined division of labor. In the highlands, the person who performs the jaca shoqpi diagnosis is the *entendido(a)*, whereas the *curandero(a)* can both diagnose and cure disease. The entendido does not have an office to see patients but accommodates himself or herself to the circumstances and conditions that a given case may present. The entendido(a) is what Barahona (1982:151), based on his observation of four healers in a highland community in Ecuador, calls *sobador de cuy* (the one who rubs with cuy). The curandero usually sees patients in his own house where he may have

Patients bring their own cuys, plants, eggs, and wax candles to the session with a curandera(o). The wait can be several hours.

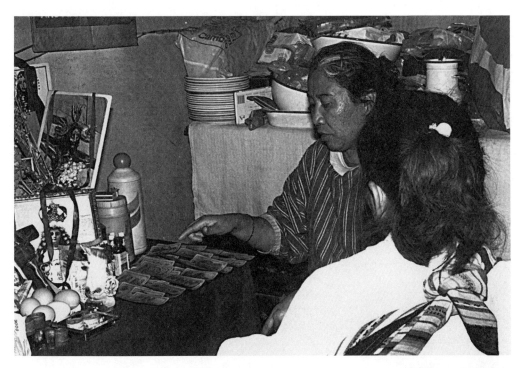

A *curandera* in Lima, Peru, reads cards for a customer. Reading cards is usually a first step in getting treatment for an illness.

a room reserved for his healing practices; regardless of the setting, patients always come to the curandero rather than the curandero to his patients. In some communities in the highlands of Peru either the entendida herself or someone else chews coca to reinforce the healing power of the cuy. In other areas where jaca shoqpi is the practice, the procedure has slight differences. The presence of an altar with a crucifix as well as the saying of prayers give the healing method a sense of religious sacrifice, where the cuy is but a medium through which the patient is diagnosed and cured supernaturally (by God).

In the practice of jaca shoqpi, soba con cuy, and cuypichay, both the curandero and the patients must meet certain requirements and conditions. In some cases the cuy should be light-colored and younger than three months, which coincides with the age at which the first estrus and adulthood occur. Patients must follow instructions about their behavior and a recommended diet for three days to one week. They must not shake hands with anyone or take showers for three days following the healing ritual. Noncompliance with the conditions by the patient brings about one consequence: the healing may not have the expected effect, or the illness or spell may be transferred to the curandero's body. Patients do follow instructions; otherwise the curandero may scold them on their next visit. If the *limpia* (cleaning) session requires the use of alcohol, perfumed water, and cuy, the patient is confined at home. Patients, especially those who hide their belief in traditional medicine, fake fractures or dislocations of their right hand to avoid shaking hands. Others are open about their faith in curanderos. Curanderos themselves go to their teachers or other curanderos whom they judge to be more powerful to get "cleaned" at least twice a year.

I will illustrate some of the differences in the three methods of

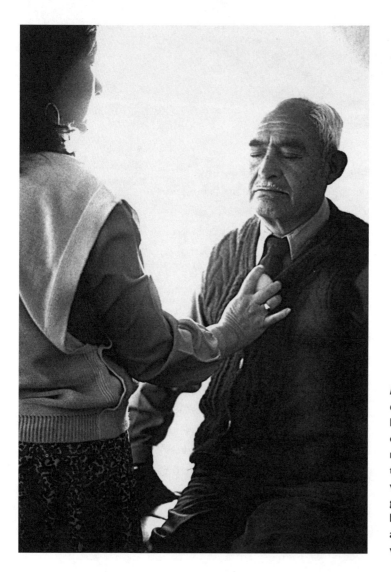

A well-respected folk doctor in Cuzco who holds a B.S. degree in biology uses eggs to diagnose disease rather than the cuy because she is a vegetarian. She accepts grains, tubers, vegetables, and fruits or cash as payment for her services.

healing I have described, with descriptions of two cases of healing in Ecuador and two cases in Peru, four of the many cases I have observed during fieldwork.[2]

Lluico (diminutive for Luis) is a ten-year-old boy who works on Saturdays and Sundays carrying dry adobes on his back for one kilo of brown sugar. Lluico has been having frequent nightmares and is very nervous. His mother believes that Lluico has *susto* (fright) folk illness.[3] I suggested that the mother take Lluico to the local medical post so that the nurse in charge could prescribe appropriate medication for him. (There are no medical doctors in this town. The closest city with some medical facilities is four hours away by car.) The mother looked at me askance and said that her friend Antonia could do as good a job as any doctor, if not better. The next day Antonia showed up along with a friend who chewed coca and smoked cigarettes for her during jaca shoqpi sessions. The jaca shoqpi took place in the yard of Lluico's home, which offered a sense of privacy, a necessary ingredient to avoid *takpa* during the healing session. Takpa is any interruption in the session which destroys the concentration of the entendida or

This man in Lima, Peru, resorted to a curandera after having visited a medical clinic for almost three months. Here the curandera is rubbing the patient with an egg to diagnose his illness. The patient holds a crucifix. He was skeptical until after three sessions when his nervousness was "cleaned" with the use of a black cuy.

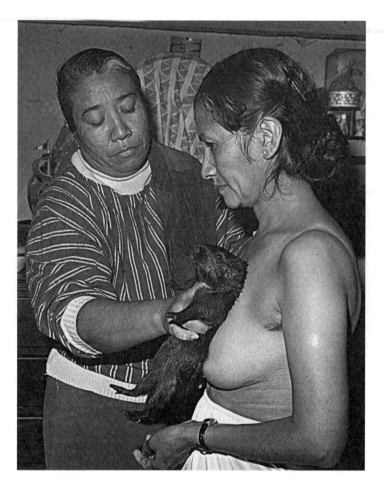

This curandera's healing method always implies a direct contact between the cuy and patient. The cuy squeaks every time it comes in contact with a part of the patient's body where there is pain or illness. Because she sweats profusely during the session, the curandera keeps a piece of cloth on her shoulder.

curandera, thus interfering with the healing power of the cuy. People who participate or observe the jaca shoqpi are expected to remain in the room for the duration of the treatment.

Antonia unfolds her shawl and spreads it onto the floor; she then places a handful of flowers on the shawl and asks her friend to sit and chew coca. The little boy lies on the floor and the session begins. Antonia passes the bunch of flowers all over the little boy's body to *shoga* or *shogay* (calm down, relax the immaterial part of the body) and to fend off evil spirits.[4] Antonia rubs the backside of Lluico's body from head to toe with the cuy. Then she tells Lluico to turn around so she can rub his face, chest, arms, and fronts of his legs also. After about ten minutes of having Lluico lying on the floor, Antonia gently sits the boy up and continues rubbing him. The last minutes of the shoqpi involve application of the cuy to the parts of the body (head and trunk) that are more vulnerable to the cold and heat as causes of illness. At the end of the procedure

Antonia grabs the cuy by its head, stands its hind legs on the floor, and cuts the animal's throat. She holds the dead cuy head down to ease bleeding, then skins it from neck down. The skinning is done so perfectly that the entire pelt remains attached to the hind legs only. Unlike other curanderos elsewhere in the Andes she does not slit the skin.

Now, Antonia submerges the skinned body along with the fresh pelt, still attached to the hind legs, in a bowl of fresh water. The flesh begins to tremble and a thin white membrane shows on the back. The trembling of the flesh and the thin white membrane indicate that the cuy has taken off both the susto and the cold from Lluico's body. Antonia examines the inner organs of the cuy and shows the mother how enlarged the heart is. This indicates inflammation of the patient's heart, which may have been caused by either ingesting food classified as hot or by too much exposure to the heat of the sun. Antonia declares the boy to be cured from the cold and susto. She prescribes ingestion of more *fresco* (cold) food. Her prognosis is that ingestion of fresco food will not result in another cold, for the lungs are affected more by the cold *viento* (night draft) than they are by food classified as cold. She recommends that to complete treatment the boy be taken to a well-

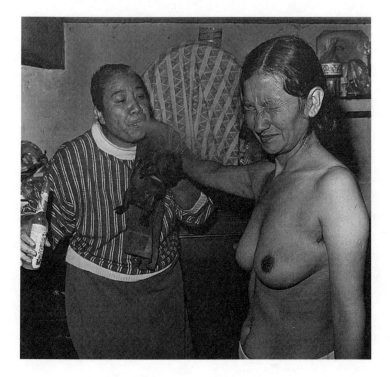

The curandera sprays perfumed water (*agua florida*) on the patient to fend off any illness after treatment. The patient holds the cuy that has died in the healing.

Both the curandera and the patient face the altar, holding the sacrificed cuy. The curandera says a prayer.

known curandero who lives in a nearby village.[5] I suspect, and I can surmise from Antonia's facial expression and her words, that one of the reasons for referring them to another curandero is that my presence in the session may have interfered with an otherwise normal procedure.

Following the healing ritual, it is Antonia's responsibility to dispose of the sacrificed cuy properly. A prescribed etiquette of disposal is strictly followed. This etiquette consists of carefully replacing the skin on the body exactly as it was before the skinning. Once the skin is replaced, Antonia wraps the carcass, along with the bunch of flowers used to shogay the patient's body, with a piece of paper. She rolls her shawl to tie it on her back and leaves for home, holding in her hand the packet containing the healing mediums. On her way home, Antonia must dispose of the packet without being noticed by anyone. I follow her closely. We come to a creek and she spots a big agave. She decides to drop the packet between the fleshy, thorn-edged leaves of the plant from which even vultures may have a hard time removing the cuy carcass.

This healer begins by rubbing the patient's body first with fresh flowers, then with the cuy.

To reinforce the healing power of cuy, the healer has another woman (right) chew coca for the duration of the healing session. The healer must dispose of the cuy properly after the healing session. She wraps the cuy carcass and the flowers she has used in a piece of paper. She will dispose of them in some isolated and distant place.

Upon disposal of the packet, Antonia and I depart in opposite directions. She continues hiking the high hills to reach her home, and I return to town. One condition Antonia and I agree on and are expected to comply with is that each of us should go home without turning back for any reason whatsoever. The folk rationale behind this belief is that turning one's head back causes what is called *tikrapay* (come back to you); that is, the illness that the cuy absorbed from the patient could come back to the person who has disposed of, or witnessed disposal of, the healing packet.

Marquez-Zorrilla (1965:135) reports that in the Conchucos Valley there was in the 1930s a healing practice known as *feyupatsa*

(spots or areas of earth that can cause fright or pregnancy or dis-
figure unborn babies). The most effective method to cure the feyupatsa was the *feyupatsa jaca shuqma* (another word for shoqpi), which
consisted of rubbing the patient with a black male cuy. In the
twelve years I have been visiting the area, I have not found nor
heard of any such healing practice in the Conchucos Valley, not
even in the town that Marquez-Zorrilla mentions to be famous for
its witches. However, the feyupatsa, under different names, is a
belief that is relatively widespread in the Andes.

In the summer of 1990, I tracked down a curandera who diagnoses and treats illnesses and fends off black magic using cuy. Pre-
suming that the curandera would not be willing to be interviewed
and observed, let alone photographed, I went to her office as a
client for an initial consultation. The curandera, named Doña
Onelia, her husband, and an adopted daughter live in a one-room
studio in one of the many old adobe tenement quarters in Lima.
In the approximately 120-square-foot living room, the curandera's
husband receives patients, sells fresh eggs and *agua florida* (perfumed water), and collects his wife's fees. The husband asks patients about the nature of their ailments and the kinds of diagnosis
or treatment they prefer or can afford. Once they are screened,
patients walk up to the penthouse where Doña Onelia sees patients. Since my interest was only to make the first contact with the
famed curandera, I decided to ask her to read cards for me. This
type of consultation facilitated a conversation around my "present
and future problems, my career, and love life." After about thirty
minutes of conversation and discussion about my research interest, she agreed to be photographed on any Tuesday or Friday, days
when she diagnoses and cures with cuy. She also suggested that I
bring my own patient and cuy to make the session more objective.

To find a person willing to undergo the diagnosis and treatment
session was no problem at all. Bertha, a woman from a *barriada*
(shanty town) near the International Airport welcomed my proposal. The difficulty was finding a black cuy that would match the
patient's sex. Even in commercial farms whose flocks number in
the hundreds, a black cuy is a rarity. If found, each cuy sells for at
least U.S.$3.50, or about 5 percent of a minimum monthly salary.
In many instances farmers and households choose to keep their
black cuys for their own use. This traditional folk healing practice,

like most Andean religious rituals, is a mix of the Catholic religion and paganism.

On the day arranged for the healing procedure, the curandera explained what was going to happen to the patient who held a black cuy on her palms. Doña Onelia began the session by saying a prayer, and the patient faced a small altar. The patient took off her clothes while the curandera put agua florida in her own mouth and sprayed it over her body. The patient looked around to make sure that I was photographing rather than filming the session. A Polaroid test print eliminated her doubts. Doña Onelia took the cuy gently and rubbed the patient's body from head to toe until the cuy died.

Now the curandera skinned the dead animal from its neck down. She slit the dead cuy to see the condition of the patient's inner organs and started telling the patient of her ailments, all of which the patient acknowledged. The cuy's left forward and hind legs and reproductive organs presented severe signs of inflammation. Doña Onelia explained to Bertha some of the symptoms of this kind of ailment, such as the pain in her left breast. She could not, however, clearly determine the cause of the inflammation. Doña Onelia recommended that two more sessions were necessary to cure the patient. The patient agreed to pursue her treatment, and we met again on Tuesday afternoon of the following week. A few days after the second meeting, the patient claimed to feel better and even began referring her friends and acquaintances to Doña Onelia (see Table 3.1).

In June of 1991 I went to visit Bertha, but she had moved to the northern outskirts of Lima. Luckily, during one of my many visits to Doña Onelia, I met Bertha's younger brother who had come to have Doña Onelia read cards for him. While he would not allow me to be present in the consultation room, he did give me his sister's new address. I went to visit Bertha on a Sunday afternoon to ask her about her health. The pain in her left breast was gone, and she had gained weight and was having a healthy pregnancy. She claimed that had it not been for "her luck in meeting me" she would still be sick and spending her money on ineffective medicine.

In the summer of 1992, in my quest to find an indigenous community in Ecuador where I could live for a few days to observe

Table 3.1 List of Some Diagnostic Signs Manifest in the
Skinned Cuy

Illness in the Patient	Signs in the Cuy
Cold	A white, thin film covers the back
Bronchitis	A white, thin film covers the back and there are fine lines of blood, like broken veins
Sore throat	Clotted blood in the neck
Diarrhea caused by cold and colic	Intestines have air bubbles and feces are sparse
Diarrhea caused by irritation	Intestines dark red or purple
Intestinal fever	Red, bloody intestines
Susto (fright)	The carcass put in fresh water trembles Shiny, whitish and glassy bowels
Witchery	Yellowish eruptions in the neck that when poked, look like pus

and photograph families and their daily activities, I met a European agronomist who had been living in the country for more
than ten years and who was a member of the staff of the experimental project described in chapter 1. The agronomist himself had
undergone treatment with cuy a few months before I met him. He
confided in me that his family life got better and his case of typhoid fever was gone thanks to his treatment with cuy. He had
visited a curandero at the suggestion of his wife. Knowing that I
was interested in every aspect of the cuy culture, he volunteered
to introduce me to the curandero who lived in Chambo, a small
town about five kilometers south of Riobamba. When I arrived at
the curandero's house, two women whose clothes smelled of a
combination of alcohol, perfumed water, and herbs were coming
out of the house. The curandero's wife reminded the women that
their next session would be the following Friday. It was late in the
afternoon and Juan Carhua, the curandero, seemed to be about to
take a siesta. Juan's wife greeted the agronomist and asked him
about his wife and children and his work.

The curandero came out from his bedroom rubbing his eyes.
He invited us to come in and sit in an empty room that he used as

Don Juan Carhua, a famed curandero of Chambo, Riobamba, Ecuador, and his pet monkey. Of necessity, he visits a "higher" curandero in the rain forest every six months so that he can be cleaned.

a waiting area. The two women we saw leaving the house had been the last patients for the day. After being formally introduced, I explained my project and my need to observe and photograph him. He understood my position and said that he would not have any problem with being photographed during any of his sessions. When I asked him whether there would be any problem with the patients' privacy, his answer was that he would handle that and that I should not worry about it. He suggested that I come back any Tuesday or Friday when he treated patients. Mondays, Wednesdays, and Thursdays were reserved for consultations. He also suggested that I bring my own black cuy in case there was no patient seeking treatment with cuy.

On my second visit I accompanied a European researcher who wanted Juan Carhua to forecast his financial and romantic future. He asked the patient to rub his body from head to toe with the wax candle he had brought. (In Ecuador reading a wax candle fire is a common practice of divination.) The curandero "saw the European researcher's problems in the *esperma* (wax candle)" and recommended he undergo a *limpieza* (cleaning). The limpieza could

Don Juan Carhua diagno-
ses an illness using a
black cuy.

be done with cuy or herbs that the curandero's wife sold in the
house. He emphasized, however, that the limpieza could be performed by any curandero if he so wanted. The European researcher decided to go to another curandero for a second opinion,
after which he sought a *cura* (healing), not just a limpieza, with a
shaman in the rain forest.

Since Juan Carhua had welcomed my observing and photographing him on any of the two days he diagnosed and cured, I
visited him for the third time. At this point I had gained his trust
and put him at ease, and he, his family, and many of his patients
were already familiar with my presence and my photographic gear.
I arrived in the curandero's house at about 8:30 A.M. and found
both the lounge and the porch crowded with patients who had
traveled for as long as six hours by car. Among them were patients
who had left Guayaquil at midnight in order to beat the crowd. I
counted forty-nine people altogether, including patients and companions. As I walked into the waiting room, one of the patients

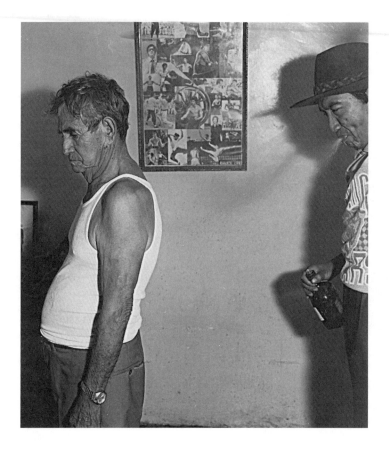

Don Juan Carhua sprays
the patient with alcohol
before and after rubbing
him with the cuy.

told me that I would be sitting there until at least 3:00 P.M. because I was the last one to come in, to which another patient whom I had seen before responded, "He is not a patient. He is making a documentary on Don Juanito's work for a local television." Soon after this patient's statement, people were eager to appear on television to attest to the effectiveness of Juan Carhua's gift. (I never told them that I was taping for television; they assumed this because of the size and shape of my medium format camera that resembled a video camera.)

Making patients wait for as long as it takes to start the healing session seems to be part of the ritual. The curandero and his wife had gone to the market and come back at about 9:30 A.M., after which the curandero had his breakfast, which had been cooked by one of his children. At about 10:00 A.M. the curandero's wife opened the window of a small room right across from the lounge and patients swarmed it. Eggs, herbs, flowers, perfumed water, and wax candles used to heal are sold on the premises, although some patients bring their own. Finally, the curandero opened the door of his treatment room and called in the first patient. An old man was prompted by his son who had driven him from Guayaquil. The curandero directed me to enter the treatment room through the back door. The elderly man removed his shirt, and the curandero closed his eyes, as if he were meditating, for about one minute. (Female patients are treated with their clothes on.) He held the black cuy gently and sprayed perfumed water on the patient's body and began rubbing him. The patient was declared to have been cleaned from "bad humor he had absorbed somewhere from someone." Each healing session took about fifteen minutes for a fee of 5,000 sucres, equivalent to U.S.$3.30 (see Table 3.1).

The use of the cuy in Andean traditional medicine also has deep mythological roots. The use of earth's natural elements by man is a privilege that must be duly acknowledged. The healing power assigned to the cuy is both a means to communicate with nature and to make an offering in exchange for a favor or request, or to appease nature's wrath. Bastien (1987) describes meticulously how small populations subsist and maintain social cohesion through rituals and practices centered on nature. He demonstrates that each and every group has a designated shrine in a mountain, which is metaphorically anthropomorphic in shape and behavior. Interpretation of the mysteries of the anthropomorphic behavior of nature is in the hands of specialized men such as altomisayocs, yachacs, llatiris, and curanderos. There are, in the far reaches of the northern Andes vestiges of a pantheistic view of the world, especially in healing with cuy.

Salasacans of Ecuador call the highest elevation in the community Quinchi Urco. It is at the foothills of Quinchi Urco where Corpus Christi dancers congregate before they descend to Pelileo, a town that lies about 5 kilometers east of Salasaca. It is the spirit of Quinchi Urco who heals illnesses caused by nature.[6] Salasacans resort more to curanderos than to scientific medicine, despite the fact that they are almost within walking distance of the fourth largest city in the country. In fact, even the community medical doctor, who is a native of the area, encourages people to seek treatment with a curandero of their preference. Further, mestizos from nearby cities and towns come to Salasaca to see curanderos. As is the case throughout the Andes, patients always bring their own

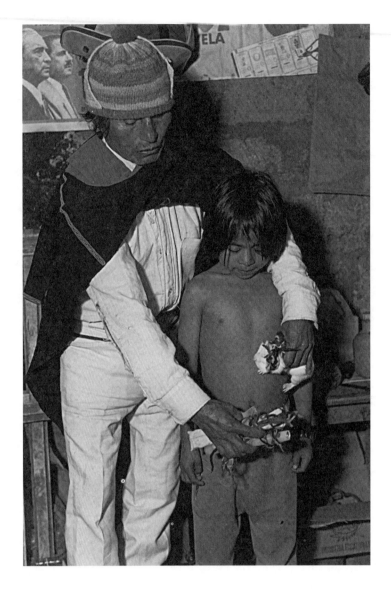

This curandero in highland Ecuador often works with an herbalist shaman who comes from a lowland community. The healing mediums (cuys, rocks, plants, and bones) may symbolize the Andean man's attempt to maintain a balance with nature.

cuys. Here there is a curandero whose singular healing practice has overtones of native religion.

Marcos Quishuar is a curandero who claims to have learned his healing skills in his youth from other curanderos in the community. This curandero heals with small rocks, a bone that he collected from Quinchi Urco, and a cuy. On a small table in one corner of the room he keeps his healing paraphernalia. A thin bone of about nine inches in length, bundled with a small piece of cloth, colored strings, yarn, and ribbons, represents the Quinchi Urco and is used in conjunction with the cuy to cure susto and illnesses caused by natural forces such as the rainbow. Parents bring their children to this curandero when they have been frightened by the earth or the rainbow. The sick child is rubbed with one of the rocks, the bone, and the cuy over and over for as long as the curandero deems necessary. The cuy does not die during the process as it does in other instances, for the death of it prognosticates death of the patient.

The parent or guardian brings an unwashed cloth or diaper that the sick child has been wearing for the last day or so. The curandero covers the cuy with the child's cloth as if he were draping a doll, which he then fastens with ribbons and yarn of various colors. The parents' or relatives' mission is to take the cuy that has absorbed the susto from the child's body to Quinchi Urco and abandon it there. While the healing can be accomplished at any time on Tuesdays or Fridays, it is recommended that the ceremonial cuy be dropped in the mountain late in the evening or night. Quinchi Urco (nature) is appeased and, whatever happens to the cuy, the susto goes back to where it came from. Ecologically, leaving ceremonial cuys in Quinchi Urco may contribute to the existence of wild cuys that are herded by the spirits of the community's ancestors that dwell in the mountain. Again, this is similar to pago practices that take place in the communities in the southern Andes, except that pago is an offering of coca leaves and food.

The use of the cuy, or parts of it, in healing is not always reserved to the exclusive realm of specialized men and women. People who are knowledgeable about folk medicine often recommend the therapeutic characteristics of the cuy to cure minor illnesses or symptoms of illnesses for which scientific treatment does not exist or is unknown. In the Cochabamba province of Bolivia some people believe that soaking one's hair with cuy broth prevents or reverses hair loss. When I walked into a traditional restaurant to order a chanka de conejo (see chapter 2), the owner wanted to know whether I was going to use the broth as medicine on myself. As I tried to ask her questions about her indirect suggestion that I soak or rinse my hair with cuy broth, she called one of her two employees to show the therapeutic attribute of the cuy broth. The owner claimed that when in January of 1990 Martina, who had migrated from Sucre to Cochabamba, was hired as a cook in the restaurant she had a dry scalp and was losing her hair. Martina rinsed her hair with cuy broth every time she washed her hair. In June 1990 when I did fieldwork in Bolivia, Martina had a thick braid whose length passed her waistline.

A few years ago folk belief attributed the existence of a sty on one or both eyelids to be behavioral rather than biological. People, especially boys who peeped through the cracks of doors or walls and those who intentionally or accidentally saw intimate parts of a woman's body, would get a sty on their eyelids. In some isolated communities the best medicine to dissolve sties was, and to some extent still is, fresh, warm cuy manure. As soon as the cuy dropped its manure the person who had a sty would pick one dropping, smash it quickly with his finger tips and apply it on the eyelid.

Among the Aymaras of the Titicaca Plateau the blood and some inner organs of the cuy are used in folk medicine to cure jaundice, rheumatism, arthritis, and chapped skin. Giving a patient the whole gallbladder of the cuy to swallow, followed by some kind of herbal brew, will cure jaundice. Likewise, drinking fresh blood mixed with sweet wine cures rheumatism and arthritis. If someone has chapped skin, common in the Andes because of the exposure to high altitude cold and sun and lack of wearing shoes or gloves, cuy fat is heated over a grill or wax candle and applied on the affected parts of the skin. The chapped skin will heal in a few hours. The gallbladder, blood, and fat that are to be used to heal must be removed the moment that the cuy is eviscerated (Ayala-Loayza 1989:118).

The Aymaras also use cuys to cure typhus. They kill two cuys and open the bodies to show viscera. They sprinkle incense and powdered herbs on the viscera, place one cuy on each foot, and bundle and wrap the patient's feet with rags. Immediately after wrapping each foot, they place one hot brick or slate on each foot. The application stays on the patient's feet until a rotten odor comes out from it, at which point the application is removed and the patient rests in bed for one day (Lira 1985:77). To dispel (despachar) an epidemic disease such as smallpox or typhoid fever, Aymaras grab their best cuy and place it under the patient's armpit for a few hours to give the cuy enough time to absorb the illness from the patient. They take the "sick animal" to an intersection, pathway, or the field where children play and drop it there so that someone can pick the cuy up and take it home. The belief is that the epidemic goes with the cuy and, obviously, is transmitted to the person who picked up the animal (Ayala-Loayza, 1989:119). This, however, does not mean that the cuy takes the disease away. This rather inhumane use of the cuy is known as *troka* (cf. Bolton 1979:293), which can be translated as "change." These folk household healing methods are not practiced throughout the Andes.

The healing power and ritualistic status of the cuy may have been derived from its domestication process, in that the wild cuy may have been taken as a gift from the *apus* (sacred mountains). Other animals that were not subdued to serve man were assigned other roles in man's relationship to the supernatural. For instance, the indomitable condor of the high cordilleras, because of its power to dwell in the apus, was used as a medium to purge and punish proscriptive behaviors such as adultery. In the Andes of Bolivia, the Kollawayas used to tie women who were suspected of having committed adultery to a pole posted in a place where condors preyed. If the condor spotted the woman and tried to tear her flesh, she was declared guilty of adultery and forced to kill herself by jumping off the top of a mountain. Twenty cases of adultery have been judged following this method of justice in the last fifty years (Ruiz-Calero, n.d: 112–135).

In the highlands of Ayacucho the wrath of the *wamanis* (gods) who reside in the mountains and lakes can take the shape of men or condors; and, if the rites are not carried out properly they can destroy crops and kill animals and entire families (Isbell 1974: 118). Sacrificing animals and offering food and plants are attempts to appease and be reconciled with supernatural forces. Reconciliation cannot, however, be accomplished by a direct communication between man and the supernatural. Creatures that men have received from the *apus*, *wamanis*, *aukis*, and so forth, mediate in the Andean man's communication with the supernatural. The cuy is one of these creatures that has the power to appease the supernatural. The inner organs of a cuy can augur the fate of the community or predict natural disasters that can destroy crops. For instance, Bastien (1985:80) describes in detail how Kollawayas, in one rite, nurture the earth with the blood of more than seventy cuys. The use of the cuy in folk medicine proves the fact that health delivery throughout the Andes is connected to the past, and its practice cannot be explained without referring to nature.

Chapter Four

The Cuy in Andean Ideology, Religion, and Belief

During the time of the Incas before the Spanish conquest, the cuy had a remarkable ceremonial position in religious celebrations (Garcilaso de la Vega 1953, chapter XVII). The Spanish conquistadors seem to have found celebrations of man's connection to nature to be absurd and an obstacle to their efforts to proselytize the native population of Peru. Despite the pressure from the Catholic Church and its followers, peasants continued practicing their beliefs. In light of the difficulty of obliterating the natives' worldview, and in order to maintain a needed labor reserve, the conquerors created new institutions such as *encomiendas* and *mitas* (Botero 1991:11). Thus, two cultures opposed to one another nurtured the formation of a new identity and a new ideology, both of which were essential if the Spanish were to be successful in controlling and exploiting native populations. It may have been in this context that the cuy maintained its position in rituals, gained the acceptance of the dominant culture, and on the surface facilitated cultural coexistence.

The biological miscegenation that was characteristic of the Spanish conquest also led to a cultural miscegenation: the use of cultural elements that were native to the Andes in the diffusion of the Spanish culture. In literature the iconographic recording of the native culture by Guaman Poma de Ayala and the chronicles of Inca Garcilaso de la Vega are still rich sources of information for many researchers. Likewise, in the arts mestizo painters, despite the influence of their European mentors, represented scenes and subjects that reflected their allegiance to things native. Painters of the

A painting of the Last Supper with Jesus Christ sharing a cuy with his apostles. It hangs in the convent of Santa Clara, Quito, Ecuador.

Cuzco school pictured Christ with a native face while the Quito school of painters portrayed Jesus Christ surrounded by his twelve apostles with a roasted cuy in front of him. There are four such paintings featuring the cuy as part of the Last Supper, and all of them come from the Quito school. Two paintings are signed by Miguel de Santiago around 1670; one of them is kept in the Cathedral of Cuzco, Peru, and one in the Museum of the Convent of San Diego, Quito, Ecuador. In 1802, Bernardo Rodriguez y Jaramillo painted the Last Supper on a mural in the Cathedral of Quito. An unsigned painting with the same motif is kept in the Convent of Santa Clara, Quito. On the one hand, inclusion of native cultural elements in religious paintings might have been a sincere artistic expression of painters who identified with Andean culture and society. On the other, this artistic expression might have been a subtle political strategy to diffuse the Catholic faith.

Ideologies, rituals, and beliefs still practiced in the Andes are reflective of the melding of two different cultures. This cultural meld has become the traditional culture whose emotional, idiosyncratic characteristic not only maintains to some extent pre-Columbian elements but also reveals an adherence to Western values. The traditional culture also resists change. Resistance, in many ways, is defined by non-Andean people to be deviant based on the fact that traditional values do not conform to Western standards. These sociocultural characteristics of the Andean culture surface in the use of the cuy in everyday life, community events, and religious festivities.

In the province of Antonio Raimondi, in the Conchucos Valley,[1] Department of Ancash, Peru, there is a singular traditional event that centers around the use of the cuy, the *jaca* (pronounced haka) *tsariy*. In this province, the jaca tsariy marks the beginning of the celebrations of local patron saints. Literally, jaca tsariy means "to collect cuys" (Parker and Chavez 1976). Socially, the jaca tsariy is an expressive demonstration of reciprocity and exchange with the family in charge of the celebrations of the patron saint's day. As communicative, expressive action (Leach 1976:9), in some communities this festivity is a play that satirizes the Spanish culture, especially the legal and social structure imposed upon native Andeans. In other communities the festivity is, in fact, a collection of donations consisting of rabbits, goats, sheep, and chickens but more importantly, and ideally, cuys.

As early as one month before the celebrations of the patron saint's day, the *mayordomo* or *prioste* (sponsor) bakes round, twisted loaves of bread, biscuits, and sponge cakes, and brews chicha to give out to female friends and neighbors. The mayordomo makes a list of the women who might make good *llumtsuys* (daughters-in-law) and appoints a *sirvinti*, a word in regional dialect for the Spanish *sirviente* (serf or attendant). The sirvinti is responsible for keeping the list of cuy donors as well as for overseeing the provision of food and alcohol, and making sure that guests are attended to according to the social etiquette that corresponds to each and

Migrants from a small town in the province of Antonio Raimondi, Ancash, Peru, who reside in Lima observe the day of their patron saint in a one-day festival. A woman dances holding a big pan containing fried cuys.

every guest's status. The sponsor sends a small basket containing baked goods and a jar of chicha along with a card appointing the would-be llumtsuys. Llumtsuys are appointed in rank and order. The first llumtsuys in rank are called *mayor llumtsuy* (the eldest daughter-in-law) and *menor llumtsuy* (youngest daughter-in-law), and the rest simply llumtsuys. If the sponsor is conscious of the local social stratification, which is more the case in relatively modernized highland towns and cities than in small villages, he appoints the llumtsuys in order of prestige from the primer llumtsuy (first daughter-in-law) to, say, twentieth llumtsuy. Whichever method of designation is adopted, women who are selected for the group of llumtsuys feel honored and rarely realize the sponsor's social bias. The mayor llumtsuy, or the first llumtsuy in her turn, recruits her own companions, appoints her own *jaca-toreros*

The *jaca tsariy* is part of a religious festival during which cuys are collected for a feast. The festival is unique to some communities in the province of Antonio Raimondi, Ancash, Peru. The *chacuas*, the man in the center who is dressed in women's clothes, is the only "woman" seen in the romping crowd.

(cuy toreros) for the night of the jaca tsariy, and reserves her best cuy for the event. Some llumtsuys do not appoint toreros; they hold their cuys themselves.

The jaca tsariy romp is a segment of the festival in which the people observe traditional etiquette. These observances vary with the social class of the prioste, who chooses the mayor llumtsuy. The llumtsuys and their jaca toreros come out for the romp without too much elaborate organization or dressing up for the occasion. Local middle-class llumtsuys and their toreros dress in peasant garbs. The primer llumtsuy and the segundo llumtsuy of the jaca tsariy of December 6, 1992, were a wealthy woman and the wife of a local merchant, respectively. The two llumtsuys had their daughters and other local girls dressed in colorful traditional woolen skirts, hats, and blouses and had special torero costumes made for their jaca toreros. To try to give the group a homogenous look, the prioste, his relatives, and his friends dressed down in worn-out hats or put old ponchos on top of their western clothes.

Early in the evening, two days before the patron saint's day, the sponsor serves the comun micuy (food served to the community). The sponsor of the upcoming year's festivities comes with as many friends and relatives as possible to the comun micuy. Here the tradition is to present the sponsor-to-be with large loaves of bread in

The giving of cuys during the *jaca tsariy* romp is a symbol of both personal reciprocity and community support.

the shape of doves, babies, or crosses. Thus, the comun micuy marks the beginning of the night of the jaca tsariy or romp (the beginning), as it is called in some communities in the province. The sponsor, along with his own musical band, leaves for the llum-tsuys' houses to invite them to join him in the inauguration of the festivities. The mayor, or first llumtsuy, is always the first one to be invited to join the sponsor and his group. Then they all go to each and every llumtsuy's door to dance and whistle to the rhythm of the songs played by the band and to drink chicha, alcohol, and *huarapo* (fermented sugarcane drink). The llumtsuys come out of their houses proudly holding a tray of cuy meal (*jaca pichu*) and

A cuy donor for the *jaca tsariy* dances while holding her cuy. In many parts of the northeastern Andes of Peru, in sexual allusions, the word jaca means *raka* (vagina). Thus, the cuy is also used to reveal the attitude that Andeans have toward sex and women. Here one of the figures of the jaca tsariy, the rucu, is flirting with the woman, saying, "Chawa (live or raw jaca) tastes better."

showing an elegantly adorned live cuy held by an appointed to-rero. (Even if the llumtsuy's offering is a live animal other than cuy, her tray always consists of cuy meal.) The sponsor then welcomes them with firecrackers, and the band begins playing a marchlike song that indicates the departure for another llumtsuy's house. The jaca toreros go dancing alongside the llumtsuys, and from time to time they place their bull (cuy) on the floor to scare people. The cuy is tied to the torero's hand with a cord or ribbon. This is done over and over until the last llumtsuy joins the crowd and they all go to the sponsor's house. In some cases, llumtsuys may number as many as one hundred, making it impossible for

A *jaca torero* boy holding his cuy during the *jaca tsariy* romp.

the sponsor to visit every house. The llumtsuys show up in the sponsor's house or they organize in small groups to meet the crowd at designated points before arriving at the house.

Once in his house, the sponsor introduces an aficionado master of ceremonies who stands by the door of a makeshift chapel ornamented with fresh fruits, bread, colorful quilts, and always the head(s) of the bull(s) slaughtered for the festivities. The llumtsuys place trays and gourd dishes containing various meals, each of which has at least one fried cuy, on a table in the makeshift chapel. To the llumtsuys' ceremonial contribution, the sponsor's sirvinti hands chicha in a gourd bowl or a drinking goblet, and a shot of anisette or alcohol. Once all the llumtsuys have displayed their

cooked cuys, the aficionado master of ceremonies appoints a judge, an attorney general, a physician, and witnesses to read the will of the deceased, which the *jaca pichus* (cuy dishes) represent. The aficionado master of ceremonies picks a jaca pichu and calls the dead cuy by the name of a local authority, politician, or anyone whom the master of ceremonies wants to satirize. He then summons the judge, the attorney general, and the witnesses for them to declare the death of a nearby hacendado, say, and to legitimate the terms of the will. The physician declares the death of the person whom the cuy represents and turns the body of the hacendado over to the witness, who hands it to the sponsor for its proper disposition. A group of women cut the cuy into pieces to serve the audience.

This satire goes on until the master of ceremonies reads the will of the last cuy. If the number of llumtsuys is too large, the ceremony of reading the wills is abbreviated in order to continue with

Only men and boys are appointed to be *jaca toreros*. Not even summer rains stopped these boys from participating in the romp.

The *jaca tsariy* is also an occasion to tease friends and political enemies. Here the "judge" appointed by the master of ceremonies pronounces that this cuy had committed suicide because "he lost the last election."

the rest of the program of the jaca tsariy. Upon disposal of the last cuy, the dance begins. During this part of the jaca tsariy, it is the role of the jaca toreros to keep the audience jolly. They do this by sneaking their cuys under the women's dresses or placing them on their laps if they are seated on the floor. At the end of the jaca tsariy, all live cuys that have been paraded in the jaca tsariy become part of the flock to be slaughtered during festivities that last for as long as eight days. (The major sponsor is responsible for the first three days of festivities. Other sponsors are charged with the rest of the festivities.)

In another town in the Conchucos Valley the jaca tsariy is different from the one I described above. The patron saint of Mirgas, one of the district towns of the province, is Santa Isabel (Saint Elizabeth), whose central day is the second day of July. The Dominguez family, one of the two sponsors of the festivities, followed the custom and etiquette prescribed by the traditions of the jaca tsariy in the province. They had invited about twenty-five families to contribute their cuys to the flock to be slaughtered for the cele-

brations. In this town, the jaca tsariy takes on its literal meaning: to collect cuys.

A high school band from another town about three hours walking distance arrives at about 6:00 P.M. At about 9:00 P.M. the sponsor, his sirvinti, friends and relatives, and the public dance in couples as if they were warming up for the long jaca tsariy night. This sort of warm-up goes on until the noise of the event attracts a loud and enthusiastic crowd of dancers, the *chacuas* (old woman), and the *rucu* (old man). The chacuas and rucu are a couple of men, one of whom is dressed in women's clothes. The chacuas carries her spinning stick with her and flirts with men she likes by smacking

Before giving their cuy dish, live cuys, rabbits, and beer that have been collected during the *jaca tsariy* romp, the llumtsuys and other donors dance in the yard of the religious officer's house.

them with it, or bumping them with her buttocks. Suddenly, even before the rucu realizes it, someone grabs the chacuas by her arms to dance with her. For the rucu it is just the beginning of a long night, for he must protect his chacuas by shoving away all men who pretend to take his woman from him.

At about 10:00 P.M. the whole group, animated by the band comprised of eighteen vigorous teenage musicians, leaves for the houses of all the families to whom the traditional invitation had been issued. The sirvinti takes a large sack along with him to collect the cuys and carry them over to the sponsor's house. (By looking at the list of cuy donors, I estimate that this jaca tsariy will last well after daybreak.) The list shows that the first family to be visited lives by the river, a walk of about fifteen minutes along narrow, muddy trails. Walkers must dodge fresh dung and large cobblestones scattered along the trail. The fact that the only means of lighting is a large kerosene lamp makes it even more difficult for me to photograph the occasion and to keep apace with the crowd, who are used to the terrain. In order to reach the first house, the group takes a short-cut through the stubble of a harvested maize crop. We all cruise through stalks, more fresh cattle dung, and many other mammals' droppings. Fortunately, the band plays a song that stimulates skipping and leaping, without missing much of the *huayno* (a popular Peruvian, Andean music) rhythm.

Finally, the romping crowd comes to a two-poled bridge, and the first house to be visited lies right on the other side of it. We all cross the bridge in single file. The sirvinti knocks on the door insistently. A drowsy woman opens the shutter to direct the sirvinti to push open the top half of the next divided door. The band plays at the other side of the bridge. The housewife complains in Quechua to the sirvinti, "You cannot take my cuys just like that. Tell your sissy musicians to dare to cross the bridge." The sponsor demands that the director of the band come into the house. The band stops playing and crosses the bridge very slowly, taking a few minutes of respite before resuming its work. The family has brewed chicha, bought one case of beer for the group, and one case of a popular soft drink for the teenage musicians. The twelve half-litre bottles of beer are finished in one round, but nobody can leave the house before the two large buckets of chicha are finished. Furthermore, the wife will not even consider handing her cuys to the sirvinti unless she sees the bucket of chicha totally empty. It is almost 11:00 P.M., and the collection of cuys has just begun. After drinking the fine, well-aged chicha, the crowd becomes a bit boisterous. The wife walks into the kitchen and comes out waving two big cuys. She drops them into the sack that the sirvinti holds wide open, and the romping and skipping group is off to the next house.

Seemingly, not even the narrow bridge deters those who want to hold and dance with the chacuas for a few minutes. But the rucu is adroit enough to cross the narrow bridge, dancing and protecting his woman. Again, the sirvinti leads the crowd to the next cuy donor. He knocks on each and every door. Some women open their doors to hand the cuy to the sirvinti, whereas others just hand the cuy through a small wall opening or shutter. The collection ends at about 2:00 A.M. At this point almost everyone is exhausted. However, the sirvinti, the chacuas, and the rucu are still lively dancers and encourage everybody to go back to the sponsor's house. Once there, the sirvinti empties the nearly full sack of cuys in the kitchen, where a group of helpers are sleeping soundly on the floor. The cuys collected during the jaca tsariy become part of the flock to be slaughtered for the banquet, which will be served to the public on the central day of the festivities.

In small towns and villages the jaca tsariy, to some extent, still maintains its regional folk characteristics. It is the beginning of the festivities of the patron saints. In populations that are going through modernization this romp is either no longer practiced or has changed considerably. Chingas is a town that in the seventies and early eighties boomed because of its agriculture and its strategic position in the smuggling of cocaine. People from the far reaches of the Huallaga Valley would walk for two days to transport goods to or from Chingas. Today, the new road that is being planned will bypass this town. It is no longer a place where goods brought in by truck or mule are exchanged. The religious cargo system has changed. When there is no prioste (religious officer), a committee collects money to pay for expenses incurred during the celebration of the local patron saint, Virgin of Mercy. The committee does not organize the jaca tsariy. Similarly, in the capital of the province, Llamellín, the celebrations of the Immaculate Conception are changing rapidly. In 1992, one of the two major priostes, who came from another province, did not organize the jaca tsariy as is the tradition. Further, a native who emigrated to Lima almost four decades ago and became a successful lawyer there was one of the two priostes in 1991. He showed up in town along with his family and his band on the eve of the central day. The jaca tsariy was not part of this sponsor's program.[2]

Migrants in Lima also observe the day of their patron saint in a one-day festival. Some sponsors do organize the jaca tsariy, serve food, and provide music to their guests, whereas others limit their responsibility to a Mass in the church and a short procession. When the festival has no sponsor, the club that represents the city or town in Lima organizes the festival and participation is limited to the people who are invited or who can afford to pay high prices for food and drinks. Many of the members of regional clubs know little or nothing about the Andean culture and tradition; to them, the term jaca tsariy may sound more foreign than Halloween.[3]

The jaca tsariy romp can be interpreted from many perspectives. For the sponsor, recruitment of the number of llumtsuys is, as in any cargo office, an indication of social prestige and wealth. The more prestige the sponsor has, the more llumtsuys he recruits and the better the jaca tsariy. In fact, some sponsors' social networks are so vast that they are unable to invite all their friends, compadres, and godchildren. Economically, the jaca tsariy is not cost effective; the amount of time and money invested and the work put into the organization of the ritual far outweigh the monetary value of live cuys and jaca pichus collected. Their symbolic value of reciprocity and exchange is more important than their monetary value. For instance, just the value of a small basketful of bread, sponge cakes, biscuits, and a jar of chicha is about the equivalent of U.S.$4, not counting the work that went into the preparation of the various foods. The live cuy and the jaca pichu are about U.S.$2.50 total. Although some sponsors are disappointed with the turnout of the number of llumtsuys, they rarely, if ever, think of the economic consequences of holding a religious office. In the ceremonial context, the use value of commodities is still considered more important than their exchange value. It is the acceptance and approval of the traditional notion of bartering and exchange, however unconscious and unequal, which ultimately weaves and nourishes the social relations between individuals and classes, as in the jaca tsariy (Mayer 1974:38).

One can also conclude that this ritual is a subtle reaction of the native culture to the imposition of Spanish values, especially in regard to the roles of the sexes. During the rule of the Incas, old people were respected and cared for, and the conquistadors preserved that value. Today in the Andes, old people are both respected and regarded as repositories of knowledge and experience. The young and the inexperienced refer to the old for help and guidance. The chacuas represents the companion of a respected old person. As such, she is expected to be virtuous and chaste, that is, abstaining from any unlawful sexual intercourse, values imposed by the Spanish. Yet the behavior of the chacuas in the jaca tsariy satirizes the ideal woman represented by the Virgin Mary. Men who seek physical contact with the chacuas, in many ways, also ridicule the fourth commandment ("Thou shall not commit adultery") by doing just the opposite. Many Andean men will say, "A fellow man's woman is even more desirable than one's own woman." The chacuas can also be a subtle mockery of the Spanish dress customs, in the sense that women in the Andes take the Virgin Mary as a model for draping their bodies. Among traditional women, wearing tight pants, short skirts, and low-necked blouses is completely disapproved of, to say the least. They still consider the Virgin Mary as the ideal model. In fact, one of the reasons women in the Andes give for resisting scientific medical help is that they cannot conceive of the idea of having their bodies examined by doctors.

Mockery using the cuy is a human invention. The cuy in and of itself cannot generate laughter. It may be charming, beautiful, hairy, fat, or ugly, but is not inherently funny. People laugh at the cuy only because they have detected in it some human attitude or expression. It is the combination of movements, gestures, and the attitudes and mental state of the people who participate in the jaca tsariy that causes laughter. When people laugh at the jaca torero or the toro, what they are making fun of is not the animal itself, but the character and the name that men have given it; that is, the cuy in the jaca tsariy has assumed a human characteristic independent of its existence as a domestic animal. Any other animal, or some lifeless object, can produce the same effect; it is always because of some resemblance to man, or the symbolic role he gives it, or the use he puts it to that causes laughter.[4] Thus, it is only when the gentle, inoffensive cuy adorned with colorful ribbons and yarns plays the role of a bigger animal (toro), or when its dark, flat, fried meat symbolizes the deceased body of an absentee landlord that the cuy contributes to the creation of laughable situations.

Other interpretations of the jaca tsariy ritual involve the role that reciprocity plays in weaving social interactions, the importance of kinship ties, and an unconscious representation of tax collection from colonial times. As an occasion to reciprocate, the officer and his collaborators observe some natural etiquette and rules. The same amount of chicha and baked stuff is handed out to every llumtsuy, as well as the community. The llumtsuys may give a case of beer or a carton of cigarettes in addition to the jaca pichu and live cuys, which may exceed the value of the officers' offering. Other llumtsuys and people from the community who were issued invitations may give what they think is "standard" or what turns out to be much less than the standard practice. The way contributions are given and the quality and amount of what is given or exchanged imply prestige for the giver, and giving less than the standard or equitable may offend the receiver (Mayer 1974:41).

Success or failure of any religious or civil event in the Andes depends on the office holder's kinship network. The incumbent officer, in most cases, saves money, stores food, and reserves livestock to meet his obligations for one year; in many instances the incumbent relies more on his kin network than on his own resources. Expectations of contributions from immediate and close relatives, distant relatives, and spiritual relatives (compadres) vary (Isbell 1974:144). Women brew chicha, cook meals to be served to the community, and see to the proper compliance with the etiquette established by tradition. Men provide wood for fuel, alcohol, music, and firecrackers. Reciprocity and reliance on the kinship network is probably the essence of the jaca tsariy, but it can also be interpreted as an unconscious representation of the collection of tributes imposed on the natives by Spanish conquistadors. Later, the church required that parishioners, especially in the countryside, contribute one-tenth of the natives' product (*diezmo*) to support the church.

The hacienda system that enjoyed the blessing of the church found subtle methods of perpetuating the position of the native

and defining the cosmology, which satisfied their personal and group interest. A symbolic representation, however typical, of the use of religious festivities to renew domination and subordination can be seen in the *rama* ritual in northern Ecuador. The rama is the practice of reciting passages from the Bible and praising and offering the hacendado a live rooster. A few decades ago the rama ritual was carried out even in haciendas owned by the Catholic Church; the rituals were performed before the priests who lived in the hacienda (Crain 1989:180).[5]

Sociologically, the jaca tsariy functions as an institutionalized

In the Imbabura province of Ecuador, during the celebrations of Saint John's Day, groups of men (*sanjuanitos*) come out to the street to drink and romp around the town plaza. The combination of rough play and alcohol usually leads to bloody fights.

method of informal social control. Mockery and ridicule are potent deterrents to deviant behavior because people place high values upon opinions of others (Elliott 1960:75). The fear of being ridiculed and gossiped about (*estar en boca de la gente*) is encapsulated in the Spanish saying "*pueblo chico infierno grande*" (small town big hell). The meaning is that in small populations secrets are rarely kept. In this sense the master of ceremonies, the judge, and the physician symbolize the values which they try to enforce. As such, they can speak for themselves or the community or their friends who may provide them with information. Thus, for instance, they can use the stage to speak for or on behalf of a friend whose wife is allegedly cuckolding. Subsequent to the jaca tsariy and other rituals, such as during the carnival, people who were alluded to usually change their behavior or are more cautious about their love affairs.

The jaca tsariy as a set of expressive social and economic behaviors can be decoded to reveal social stratification and power structure as well as complex verbal and nonverbal communication codes. Religious officers are always people who enjoy at least a relatively comfortable economy, for the office demands sizable

Throughout the Andes natives are invariably the bulk of the consumers of alcohol, and the brewers and sellers are mestizo vendors and middle-class merchants.

amounts of cash outlay. For instance, a religious officer in one of the towns of the province of Antonio Raimondi, in 1992, claimed to have spent about U.S.$5000, a sign of economic power and social prestige. Invitation to participate in the jaca tsariy (distribution of baked goods and chicha) is always issued to people of the same or higher stratum than that of the officer. Gente común (common people) spend their own money by way of "cash advance on wages" or by selling their farm products. Further, if the officer is socially sensitive enough to invite common people, he makes sure that they are served dishes specially cooked for them, such as cabbage and potatoes with pieces of ham or lamb or charqui (dried beef) and low-quality chicha, but not cuys, which says something about not only who the officeholder is but also why he is doing what he is doing.

Religious cargo officials also slaughter many dozens of cuys to make traditional dishes. For instance, the Randalls, an American couple who have been living in Ollantaytambo, Cuzco, for almost twenty years, slaughtered one cow, two pigs, three sheep,

At a Saint Peter's Day celebration in Zuleta, Imbabura, Ecuador, a landed family and their guests do not come into direct contact with the peasants. At a hacienda house former serfs offer a live rooster each to the *hacendado* and the manager (*administrador*).

and about one hundred cuys for the lunch served to friends and relatives. They also fed the community in the town's sports campground with the *chiri uchu*, a cold meal consisting of ham, turkey, sausage, cheese, parched maize, and always cuy.[6] They did this in order to comply with the customs and traditions of the Pentecost celebrations for their *carguyoc* (religious office). Compadres and friends helped the Randalls transport roasted cuy, pork, lamb, chicken, seaweed and cheese, parched maize, and ground hot peppers. In the campground, each carguyoc camps in one spot, and the helpers cut the cooked meat into bits. They begin handing out the chiri uchu in paper plates to everyone who stops by for it.

In the city of Cuzco, eating chiri uchu is similar to having the traditional turkey in the American Thanksgiving dinner. Some families cook their own chiri uchu, whereas others go to public places to buy it. The chiri uchu vendors roast cuys sometimes as early as one week before Corpus Christi. After paying their fee to the municipal government, they set up their tables and benches for customers and stack up their cases of beer and soft drinks in the block(s) or areas reserved for the fair. On the table, in a large

Pentecostal celebration in Ollantaytambo, Cuzco. For nonnative people sponsoring a religious festivity is something like becoming native in spirit. Here the religious sponsors, an American couple who have been living in the community for almost twenty years, and their friends gather in front of the church before the Mass. About one hundred cuys were cooked to serve the traditional *chiri uchu* to the community.

bowl or an earthen pot, many whole oven-roasted cuys decorated with green peppers, seaweed, and blood sausage are displayed. These decorations are either placed in the mouth of the cuy or strung on it. People go to the street fair to savor the chiri uchu for about the equivalent of U.S.$1 per serving. However, many people go to the fair more for the uninhibited environment that the chiri uchu fair creates for drinking alcohol and alcoholic beverages than to taste the traditional dish. People who are alienated from the native culture, or can afford to cook their own chiri uchu, reject the chiri uchu street environment and stay home for the holiday.

In other communities in the Andes the use of the cuy appears in a slightly different fashion but in the same general, religious context. The most important religious festivity in the community of Salasaca, Ecuador, is Corpus Christi, which lasts for approximately one month. Corpus Christi festivities in Salasaca are divided into four separate celebrations, each of which is marked by its own particular rituals. These rituals are the Ensayo, which takes place the Sunday before Corpus Christi, and the Octava, which happens

During the Ensayo the wives of the dancers are served boiled potatoes with a roasted cuy on top.

ten days after Corpus Christi. The Chishi Octava is the last day of festivities, and it takes place the Sunday following the Octava. The Salasaca Corpus Christi is a native ritual adopted from the Catholic calendar. Both Salasacas and the priests are indifferent to one another's celebrations. The local priest does not celebrate any mass, nor do the Salasacas care about the religious aspect of Corpus Christi.[7]

The community has sixteen *alcaldes* or religious officers (traditional authorities in other communities), and each alcalde is expected to participate actively in the celebration of Corpus Christi. Alcaldes contract a musician and dancers, and provide friends and neighbors with plenty of food, chicha, and alcohol, using their

In Salasaca, Ecuador, the Ensayo of Corpus Christi is a day when all the alcaldes share food with their community, reward their dancers, and reciprocate with friends and relatives who contributed food, drinks, or cash to the occasion.

own resources. Although some alcaldes do not get help from close relatives and friends, many people from the community give their *jocha* (contribution). As in any traditional group the position of alcalde carries with it prestige in the community. The four days of festivities center on watching the dancers, feasting, and drinking, with some slight changes from one celebration to another. Here I will describe only the Ensayo, for its rituals include the use of the cuy.

On the day of the Ensayo (a ritual that consists in feeding the community, especially people who contribute to or collaborate with the alcalde's successful sponsorship of religious celebrations), at about 10:00 A.M., two or three dancers and their families,

In Salasaca, the central part of the Ensayo is saying the Lord's Prayer during which people are expected to remove their hats as the man on the left has done.

a musician (*maestro*), relatives, and neighbors gather in the yard of the alcalde's house. The alcalde, his dancers, and the musician sit on stools and chairs in the middle of the yard. The alcalde greets and welcomes everyone. Once in the yard, women huddle on the floor and men join other men who are drinking or just chatting. Rarely do husbands and wives sit together. The ritual begins when the alcalde commands the musician to play his drum and *pingullo* and prompts a relative or close friend to start handing out bread and fruit to everyone in the house. The alcalde's wife in turn asks her helpers to serve the soup and *mote* (boiled corn) in clay dishes. Among Salasacas *wanlla* is a gift or food offering that visitors can take home. Women carry with them empty clay pots and dishes in order to receive their wanlla. The wanlla always consists of two dishes—bread and fruit. Women pour their soup into their clay pots and wrap bread and fruits in their shawls or put them in bags or baskets. Wanlla elsewhere can be defined as snack, treat, dessert, and junk food (Weismantel 1988:110). In some parts of Peru wanlla is known as *alsa*.

The central part of the Ensayo ritual is the offering of *mediano* (ceremonial food) to the dancers, musicians, other close collaborators, and to the community. The alcalde and his dancers sit in a row and have in front of them a wooden table on which plenty of mote and bottles of alcohol and wine or champagne (if the alcalde can afford it) are placed. At this point many men, including the dancers, are drunk, and some have already passed out and are sleeping on the floor. A community member versed in the Catholic religion prays the Lord's Prayer in Spanish, then turns his eyes to the table to preach (in the Quechua language) about how important to them *santa sara* (sacred corn) is. Every man removes his hat and pays attention to the speaker for as long as he prays and preaches. Finally, a big bowl of boiled potatoes, one live chicken, and big pieces of bread especially baked for the occasion are handed to the dancers. The alcalde's wife hands over a bowl of boiled potatoes with a whole roasted cuy on the top to the wives of the dancers, who take the offering home as wanlla.[8] Food and drink offerings are not only signs and symbols of reciprocity from the alcaldes to their friends, relatives, and neighbors, they are also indicators of power and prestige. More people go to the wealthy alcalde's house than to the poor alcalde's house.

Corpus Christi *castillos* **in Pujilí, Cotopaxi, Ecuador. A castillo is a pole to which cuys, bottles of beer, fruits, and sacks of potatoes are attached.**

In the small town of Pujilí in the province of Cotopaxi, Ecuador, and in many other small communities live cuys are used in celebrations of religious festivities. In Pujilí, Octava takes place the day after Corpus Christi. In the town plaza families and whole neighborhoods who had agreed the previous year to participate in the decoration of the plaza plant *jardines* and *castillos*. Jardines are the best plants and flowers grown in the canton (something like county in the United States), and they are placed in a circle around

Men and boys who suc-
ceed in climbing up the
castillo grab their prizes.

the castillos. A castillo, commonly known in the rest of the country as *palos encebados* (greased poles) or just as *palos* (poles), is a tall wooden structure built especially for the Octava. The organizers of the celebration tie prizes to the crossbars of the castillo, or they put the prizes in baskets that hang on the castillo. If the prizes are in baskets, it is difficult to see them from the ground.

Each sponsoring community or neighborhood puts its name written on white cloth on top of the castillo. Prizes placed on the castillo depend on the organizer's status and creativity. Thus, townspeople who enjoy a relatively comfortable economy may feature in their castillo manufactured and imported goods such as jeans, toys, small electronics, tin pots, silverware, and so forth, and very little, if any, locally produced goods. Peasants are among those sponsors whose economy is tied to agriculture; they put on their castillo local fruits and animals, in addition to some store-bought products. Organizers invariably tie as many as ten cuys on the castillo, especially white cuys. Once the castillo is planted in the ground, men, especially boys, dare climbing the pole to take a prize. Informants say that a few years ago the castillo poles were greased, which made climbing it difficult, and that there have been cases when climbers slipped down and were seriously injured or died.

In the same province of Cotopaxi, in the city of Latacunga, there is a festivity known as La Santísima Tragedia or La Mama Negra; it is celebrated twice a year, on September 24 and on the first Saturday of November. The first festivity is in honor of the Virgin of Mercy and is organized by the *vivanderas* (marketwomen). The second celebration is a civic event that commemorates the independence of Latacunga and is organized by the municipal government; participants in this event are professionals—businessmen, politicians, and so forth. People claim that the second festivity is a tourist attraction, while the first one is an authentic folkloric event. In both cases La Mama Negra is actually a parade of many groups of people dressed in costumes, and consumption of alcohol is indirectly encouraged. The central figure of the parade is the Mama Negra, a man dressed as a black woman riding a horse. Mama Negra is the climax of the parade and comes at the very end. Another attraction of the parade is the *ashangero* (the one who carries the *ashanga* on his back). The ashanga is a basket of food that is symbolically offered to the city of Latacunga. A whole roasted pig is placed in upright position in a basket. Each and every ashanga has invariably at least five roasted cuys that are pinned or tied onto the roasted pig. Ashangas weigh well over two hundred pounds each. Two men help the ashangero carry the heavy basket and two men come right behind him carrying a table on which the ashanga is placed every time the ashangero decides to rest. People who stand on both sides of the street applaud both the ashangero's physical strength and the presentation of the ashanga.

The character that attracts the public's attention is known as the *loador* (a person, especially a young male, who recites passages from the Bible, say, on behalf of the group that hired him for this purpose). His role is as an entertainer. The loador paints his face in black and wears sunglasses to conceal his identity. The verses he recites are often picaresque and are meant to ridicule the dominant class, politicians, and legal authorities. An example is, *Las mujeres de mi tierra tienen en el pupo una taza; y mas abajo tienen lo que les gusta a los Galo Plaza.* (Women from my town have a cup on their belly buttons;

and below their belly buttons they have what the Galo Plazas like.)[9]
This is intended as ridicule of the sexual behavior of one of the
dominant families in Ecuador. Throughout the country people
joke about the fact that the only reason there are so many light-
skinned peasants in Zuleta (the Galo Plazas' hacienda) is that the
Galo Plazas fathered many children.

In Latacunga, Cotopaxi, Ecuador, *ashanga* is a symbolic food offering to the city. Ashanga always consists of whole roasted pork, cuys, rabbits, fruits, and alcoholic drinks, and is served to the *jocheros* (collaborators) at the end of the festivity. The roasted pigs are attached to a bier with shafts.

Cuy in Folk Games and Beliefs

Andeans have many beliefs concerning plants and animals, and some of these beliefs are connected directly to the cuy and its behavior. In the Cochabamba province of Bolivia there is a folk game that goes on after a feast that is connected to drinking beer or thin, light chicha. This game requires two or more participants. Once celebrants finish their lunch or dinner, they nibble the fried head of the cuy and crack the skull to pick out the two tiny bones of the eardrum that are about one-eighth of an inch in size. The two bones, which people call *zorros* (foxes) because of their shape, represent the two sexes. The smaller of the bones represents a woman and the larger one a man. The two bones, submerged in chicha or beer, have divination power. The male "fox" is smudged with soot and dropped in a glass containing the alcoholic drink along with the female "fox." The part of this game that requires some skill is placing the two bones in the bottom of the glass next to each other. Before drinking the chicha or beer, they stare at the glass, close their eyes, and think of their wives, girlfriends, lovers, and so forth. They consult mentally with the "foxes" to divine the loyalty of their wives, girlfriends, or lovers. As they drink the beer or chicha they keep watching the position of the two tiny bones. If one of the foxes moves away from the other, it means that either the husband or wife, or boyfriend or girlfriend, is cheating on his or her partner. Depending on the strength of their belief, or whether the divination game corroborates their suspicion, they may also consult with a *llatiri* (sage).

In Peru, the use of the two "foxes" is known throughout the country, especially in urban areas where bars and chicherias are found on almost every block. Picanterias are popular in sections of cities or settlements where highland migrants or working-class people are concentrated. The name of this game is *sacar el zorro* (to remove the fox from the glass), and it may take place in a private home or in a restaurant where the cuy dish is served. The game does not have any divination power. It is rather a drinking challenge that leads to drunkenness and quarrels or even fistfights. The object of the game is to remove the "foxes" from the glass. The challenger drops the bone into the glass and dares others to drink

This Peruvian woman sold her cuys to take cash to the Qoillur Riti festival. She rests and chews coca after having walked for four hours to the mountain where the festival takes place.

up the wine, beer, or chicha and slide the bone out. As they tilt the glass the bone either remains in the bottom of the glass or slides down a little bit but not enough to touch the lips. Various challengers try repeatedly with no success. It is always agreed upon that each failed attempt to remove the bone from the glass implies buying a round of drinks to match the number of bottles of beer or glasses of wine with which the game started. The challenger is almost always someone who is skilled in the trick of removing the zorro. Therefore, he may drink for many hours, spending little or no money at all.

I have a final example of folk belief about the cuy. I was coming home after a three-month visit in the northeastern highlands of

In Cuzco, as many as 10,000 people go to a mountain to pay homage to the Señor de Qoillur Riti; the event coincides with the celebrations of Corpus Christi. Pilgrims hike for about four hours to reach the mountain where celebrations take place. They carry with them food provisions including well-spiced roasted cuys.

In Peru, peasants traveling long distances take along their cuy *fiambres*.

Peru. To reach the point where motorized transportation was available I had to hike for about six hours. Since I had left the village where I was doing fieldwork late in the afternoon, I was still about two hours away from my destination when it began to get dark. A middle-aged woman, who on other occasions had offered me shelter, encouraged me to spend the night at her house and resume my hike early the next morning. When I told her that I was equipped to hike by night, she said that I would not reach my destination that night because the trail would be slippery. "Two of my cuys have been coughing for almost two hours," she said. "Furthermore," she continued, "can you not see all those big, ominous gray clouds?" After having potato stew with chunks of smoked ham and a thick wheat soup, I decided to stay. In fact, about one hour after dinner, when we were telling ghost and witch stories, it began drizzling. In some communities in the southeastern Andes when the cuy stands on its hind legs and demonstrates a whistling, coughing-like sound, people believe that it is a sign of bad luck and a prediction of death in the family. In this case the animal is killed and cooked immediately (Ayala-Loayza 1989).

In the northeastern Andes, long-distance travelers bring back home the sculls of their cuys as part of their *fiambre* (cooked food provision to last for many days). The belief is that if they do not do this there will not be enough cuys in the household livestock for the next trip. Other long-distance travelers keep the right foot of the cuy as an amulet with which to walk without getting tired and for good luck. Others who cross high mountains that are believed to be the dwellings for the *ahuilus* (Quechua word for spirits of the ancestors) try to eat their cuy fiambres in these mountains, again for good luck.[10] They offer the ahuilus the skull of the cuy along with their coca quids in exchange for protection from natural forces such as rainstorms and lightning that may cause casualties or damage the goods they are transporting.

Chapter Five

The Future of
the Cuy Economy

The cuy appears to be following a path similar to that of other Andean natural resources. Potatoes, quinua, tomatoes, pepino (*Solanum muricatum*), and tree tomatoes (*Cyphomandra betacea*), to mention a few, have been adapted to other climates to benefit the economies of industrial societies (NRC 1989). Today, quinua produced in Colorado is readily available at many health stores in the United States (McCamant 1992:123), and the llama is raised in Colorado and Virginia to be used as pack animal and pet (Cain 1989:20).

The cuy that three decades ago was raised only in the traditional household kitchen in the Andes is now commercially raised in or near urban areas such as Arequipa, Cajamarca, Lima, and Huaraz in Peru; Cuenca, Ambato, Quito, and Ibarra in Ecuador; and Pasto and Cali in Colombia to meet the demand for its meat, which has increased with migration of people from the highlands to cities and towns. Even farmers in the state of New Jersey who raise cuys to satisfy the pet market in the United States are selling cuys to Andean residents in the New York metropolitan area. In time use of the cuy as a source of high protein will extend beyond the borders of Andean nations and be accepted in other societies. Thus, if properly implemented, production of the cuy for the international market may contribute to modernizing the countryside in the Andes. In the meantime, however, the likelihood is great that the cultural practices involving the cuy, including the traditional way the cuy is raised and the folklore that has grown up around the cuy, will change radically.

The fact that the cuy adapts easily to almost any altitude is an

Cuy meat is already available in urban areas in the United States. Many food vendors like these two women sell frankfurters, ethnic dishes, and barbecued cuys in public parks in New York City. Each cuy costs from U.S.$20 to U.S.$30, depending on the size.

advantage to raising it commercially, especially in areas where conditions of producing forage are favorable. Thus, it is realistic to predict that, in the long run, prepackaged cuy meat may be made available at supermarkets in industrial societies around the world. This would most certainly be an economic breakthrough and might happen in the following progression. Cuy meat would be served at ethnic restaurants in large urban areas, where hundreds of people of Andean origin live. In fact, a restaurant in one of the boroughs of New York City opened by an immigrant family already serves roasted cuys on weekends at U.S.$25 per cuy.[1] Once it has gained recognition in national economies, the low-fat high-protein cuy meat may merit consideration by the increasing number of people in industrial societies who, because of their sedentary habits, are becoming more and more conscious of their dietary practices. The expectation is that the economic advantage of using the cuy as an excellent food source will outweigh a society's sentiment concerning the cuy as household pet. When this happens, the cuy may be one more product indigenous to the Andes that will be industrially exploited and controlled by groups whose economic undertakings are either connected to subsidiaries of multinational monopolies or dependent on foreign investors, but the probability is that the economic success of the cuy as food will not benefit the people who are from the homeland of the cuy.[2]

It seems that the scientific breeding and the development of the cuy economy, such as it is, aim at controlling the material conditions of production in the Andes; that is, the governments of the four Andean countries are trying to change people's mentality that would lead to changes in the traditional methods of raising cuys (Archetti 1992:144). This effort to modernize the country-side does not include the traditional culture in the equation and puts two groups in conflict: the peasantry, who despite their desire to change cling to their culture, and the white or mestizo who strives to integrate the peasantry into the modern world. As they stand today, policies that aim at national integration do not take into consideration the peasants' social and economic condition nor do they satisfy the immediate needs of peasants. Peasants do not have the education necessary to assess their needs nor are they in a position to direct their own destiny; urban mestizos lack knowledge of and true identification with the peasantry at large. Because of the cuy's cultural and ecological connection to the Andean man, its prolific character, and potential for short-term cash yield, the cuy is a good candidate to stimulate change and supplement local economies. If programs and projects of economic development fail, the cuy will still remain in its present stage or regress to its traditional level but will not become an endangered species.

The central Andean subregion presents such ecological diversity that within a few minutes' drive or a few hours' walk one can be transported to places that have different geographical, topological, climatic, and human conditions. Some ecozones and communities have appropriate or ideal physical conditions for the production of a number of crops that may yield two harvests per year. Other ecozones are suitable only for one crop. Yet there are still others where it is difficult to sustain agriculture and animal husbandry at all. This ecological constraint on cuy raising makes it difficult to maintain flocks, especially during the dry season when feed is available only where there is irrigated land. In many communities cuy raising and feed production bring together agricultural activities. People from microregions who enjoy a year-round water supply provide other communities with forage for their cuys and other household animals. The commercial production of cuys may even bring about changes in the peasants' attitudes toward agriculture.

Cuy raising at the family level is mostly a housewife's activity, whereas middle and industrial level of production, with rare exceptions, is a male activity. Promotion of economic activities connected to the cuy seems to be effecting changes in the traditional Andean society in relation to the division of labor by gender. This latent, however seminal, desire to change an ideology that is deeply rooted in male dominance is perceived, for example, in the Proyecto Comunitario Palmira, especially in the community of Tiocajas, Chimborazo, Ecuador, where nonpeasant people trained in animal husbandry and farming are trying to transfer the knowledge and use of simple technology to better their social conditions. Therefore, because social and material conditions influence and reproduce ideology, grassroots economic development such as cuy raising may bring about significant social change in the peasantry.

The production of cuys for routine consumption or commercial purposes in the Andean subregion is not a totally new activity, but it is one that requires the application of better and more effective methods than the traditional know-how. The relative ease with which the Andean culture absorbs foreign cultural elements should be exploited by policymakers to try to integrate rural and native populations isolated from one another. Modern production of the cuy at the family or community level is a plausible strategy to be included in an economic development program that strives for integration of isolated communities. In other words, the industry of producing cuys for the commercial market must be designed in such a way to enable Andeans to become active participants in that industry. New and better breeds of cuys have been developed using scientific technology, but they have all grown out of an indigenous culture's knowledge and resources. Policymakers and the scientific community need to support the exploitation of cuys to benefit the Andean man first and foremost.

One aspect of cuy raising about which most Andean people are not familiar is the inherent risk of diseases and how to anticipate that possibility. Educating people in this regard will be a slow process, however effective, because many folk beliefs connected to the behavior of cuy will change as its use value changes in relation to its exchange value. Four economic advantages give the cuy a role of inducing changes in local economies, in attitudes, and probably in the impoverished peasant's position in the modern world. First, production costs are about 28 percent of the selling price, if production relies on both forage available in the environment and concentrated feed (Koeslag 1989:2; Moncayo 1992c:4). (The use of concentrated feed should be discouraged because people claim that the meat is less appealing to people who already know quality taste in cuy meat.) Second, a three-month-old cuy with a weight of about .800 kilos sells for twice as much as one kilo of sirloin beef (U.S.$2.10) or 46 percent higher than chicken (U.S.$1.83 per kilo). Even if an increase in supply drives prices down, producers will still earn income. Third, unlike other farm products such as wheat, potatoes, coffee, and fruits that are produced worldwide, the cuy does not have any competition in the world market. Fourth, pigs and chickens that are widely raised in the Andes for food and for cash are dependent on the consumption of barley, maize, wheat, potatoes, and even fruits and water, and are therefore in competition with human beings for their commodities. The cuy, to the contrary, thrives on forage and corn especially bred for animals.

One effective development of the cuy economy may be the inclusion of the nutritional importance and economic potential of the cuy in school curricula. Today, education in the Andes is designed to fit the urban, metropolitan needs and interests. For instance, in Peru, high school students in remote villages must take English for five years when many of them are not even fluent in Spanish. Initiatives to educate Andean people in the use of their own natural resources must come from people who, though superficially and mostly for political reasons, are connected to the subregion. Although in light of the class-biased bureaucrats that dominate international organizations this suggestion may be too quixotic, at the international level organizations such as United Nations and Organization of American States (OAS) must encourage Andean governments in the promotion of cuy meat consumption. The United Nations' participation in making Latin Americans aware of the cultural significance, economic potential, and nutritional value of the cuy is small, or even unnoticeable, and only academic in nature. This participation need not imply funding research or creating bureaucratic positions, but it should suggest symbolic motivations to develop interest for and appreciation of something that is part and parcel of the Andean culture. This token participation, however unprecedented in the long run, for instance, must take the first step to change officially the misnomer guinea pig for cuy; declare the cuy a pan-Andean patrimony; reproduce its picture in stamps and postcards; publish leaflets with facts that can inspire Andeans to be proud of their culture and heritage; and so forth.

Biotechnology has been successful in reversing the regressive method of cuy raising that people in the Andes were practicing. The Peruvian cuy is now widely raised throughout Ecuador, Colombia, and Bolivia. There is no question that the cuy can contribute to the development of sustained economies. To reach this economic stage, it is necessary that national governments consider seriously programs of technology transfer that researchers in Peru and Ecuador have gained. If the current production of about 50 million cuys was increased fivefold, consumption of cuy meat per year would increase to well over five hundred million. Local or regional economies and nutrition would experience some visible, though not substantive, changes. More importantly, the improved material conditions of the Andean man would, eventually, nourish changes in his ideas and thought processes. Changes that are imposed by people who live a totally different material life are counterproductive. An illustration of the kind of counterproductiveness that I am talking about is the United States' attempt to control the production and trafficking of coca and cocaine; that approach fails to take into consideration the Andean population and its dependence on coca for a livelihood. Policies and models of change devised and pre-packaged by bureaucrats who cannot see the Andean reality with the natives' eyes are doomed to fail. If social relations of production, to borrow a Marxist term, are maintained at *status quo*, social maladies and ideological movements will continue to rise. It is up to the groups who control *de facto* by controlling the world economy, technology, and knowledge to decide the future of marginal societies in a fast-changing world.

Appendix

Notes on Cross-Cultural Fieldwork

Social scientists—especially anthropologists and, to some extent, sociologists—are constantly involved in fieldwork in foreign cultures. Fieldwork may involve progressive insertion, or immersion, of a stranger into a community or into the lives of selected key informants, depending on the researcher's ability to interact with people of different cultures and on the type of information being collected. Fieldwork may take from a few months to many years of periodic visits in the setting that last from a few days to several months. Howell (1990:50) concludes that, on the average, academics spend between thirty to sixty days per year in the field over the course of their lives. During this time, the researcher gets involved in face-to-face interactions with people, which involve mutual perceptions that play important roles in the outcome of the fieldwork and, eventually, in the researcher's career. The conclusions of the field research are, then, based on an amalgam of images, shapes, and feelings that the fieldworker has experienced and communicated to others by describing informants' behaviors and feelings. As I reflect, based on my experience of fieldwork in the Andes, there are two issues I believe are worth discussing here: the native as opposed to nonnative researcher and the use of still photography in fieldwork.

The questions I address here are simple. What are the advantages and disadvantages of being a native or a nonnative researcher? How do native and nonnative researchers gain rapport with their subjects? Is social research in the Andes anything but an academic version of what began with the European invasion? How does the camera affect the data-gathering process? How do we deal with populations that are not used to cameras? Finally, does the use of instant pictures entice subjects who otherwise might not participate in the research process, or is the use of instant pictures a token compensation for informants' cooperation and time? In order to give my arguments a true ethnographic flavor, I will describe situations involving myself as the researcher and my informants by using detailed vignettes and anecdotes I have collected in the field for the past ten years.

The Native Stranger

By their national origin, in relation to their field of preference or expertise, cross-cultural ethnographers can relatively safely be divided into natives and nonnatives. Native ethnographers may be local researchers who look into their immediate social reality, or they may be native academics who were trained outside of their country of origin, work in foreign universities, and do research on their native cultures. Subjects or informants react differently to the presence of either type of native researcher. Among nonnatives two types of researchers can be identified: those who try to look at a foreign culture from inside by playing at being native and those who seek to be accepted by their subjects as they are. Inevitably, the subjects' reactions will depend upon many factors, such as the researcher's topic, personality, language skills, and research approach. Fieldwork is an arena where people try to capitalize on the fieldworker's need to gather data, and researchers who go to the field equipped to face challenging situations use their skills to take advantage of every possible situation that they create or encounter.

In *Webster's II University Dictionary* (1984), the third meaning of native is "belonging to, or characteristic of the original inhabitants of a given place, especially those of primitive culture." A researcher who was born among and shares biological and social traits with the researched people qualifies as a native researcher. Fluency in language, knowledge of the peoples' idiosyncrasies, and the ease of physical readaptation to the environment expedite an effective insertion or reinsertion into the culture. A native creates ethnography by living the life of his subjects and by experiencing the others' world over the lifetime of his career (Stoller 1989: 249).[1] This leads to the assumption that a native researcher has an advantage vis-à-vis his foreign counterpart; that is, the native researcher can collect data in a much shorter time than a nonnative researcher. This assumption may not be true for natives who were educated in foreign countries or are affiliated with foreign academic institutions.

The researcher's entrée into the setting always leads either to the possibility of gaining rapport with subjects or to rejection (Stoller 1989; Rabinow 1977:76). Neither native nor foreign ethnographers may rule out the likelihood of confronting those elements that may come under political, religious, or legal aegis. The researcher who knows the culture and can communicate with field gatekeepers, who are often found in traditional communities, has a better chance of being accepted and actually participating in personal or local affairs. However, too much participation could turn into advocacy, an untenable scientific position. Among traditional groups, depending on given situations, the native researcher is almost always taken as either a visitor or an intrusive person trying to capitalize on his own culture.[2] The attitude of persons in a culture under study toward nonnatives, especially Anglo-Saxons, differs radically.

Indigenous informants in traditional societies are more attracted to foreign researchers than they are to their fellow natives. I can identify two main reasons for the different treatment of native and nonnative fieldworkers. First, the colonial mentality of the Andean people puts indigenous and native informants in an unequal power position before a foreign participant-observer (Homiak 1990:2). In many ways, the Aristotelian philosophy of the sixteenth century that denied the human nature of "Indians" (Hanke 1959) is still embedded in the Latin American ideology.[3] Second, the nonnative goes through a kind of socialization process during which he is very inquisitive about many cultural trivialities. Key informants and the community feel they have a moral obligation to teach and protect nonnatives. In addition to their submissive attitude, the Andean people are extremely hospitable, especially to strangers. In this regard, one can safely state that the saying, "My house may be small but my heart is big" (*La casa es chica pero nuestro corazón es grande*) applies to people throughout the Andes. Due to these social and ideological factors, the native researcher often takes different directions such as indirect or informal interviewing that involve extensive socialization. This seems to be the most effective method of data collection, although subjects or informants may have negative opinions or suspicions of outsiders in general.

In small highland populations, people cannot conceive of the fact that people from advanced societies come to such remote places where they face so many inconveniences. Their assumption is that anyone who would make such a choice does so because he is avoiding the judicial system or is a failed or frustrated professional. When I was doing fieldwork in a community in 1981, one of the rumors that was spread in the community about me was that I was a failed professional and that I was trying to relearn life in the countryside after many years abroad. To this, people who knew of me would argue that if I were relearning life, I had no need to go beyond my hometown, for my family had enough resources so that it was not necessary for me to relearn anything. I remained impartial, for siding with either version of the rumor would have quelled the opportunity for people, especially women, to gossip on the subject.

Gossip and rumors can possibly keep the researcher's name and intention in the minds of the subjects or potential subjects.

Frequently, in participant-observation, the researcher's involvement in the informants' personal affairs or the group's collective life is intense. This involvement is at times desired to obtain or verify information (see for example, Whyte 1984; Harper 1987a, 1987b; and Williams 1989). For the ethnographer, involvement in the subject's life is a constant process of gathering information. For instance, I know of an urban ethnographer in New York who had to contact repeatedly an attorney for one of his informants who was always being arrested in drug raids. Here the ethnographer was immersing himself in his subject's life. He was not approving of his subject's criminal behavior nor was he supporting drug dealing. Sometimes subjects or groups furnish information by way of presenting their problems because they believe that an educated person will give them guidance. They do not realize that both native and nonnative researchers are there to learn and can contribute very little, if any, toward easing their everyday plights.[4]

Extended fieldwork or short fieldtrips to gain knowledge of a culture by experiencing the harsh living conditions (by American standards) also introduce difficult situations that come with the social and political conditions of the host community or country. In many areas of the Andes, especially Bolivia, Colombia, and Peru, nonnatives are more vulnerable to violence than natives. During the late eighties, for instance, doing fieldwork became dangerous for foreigners, particularly American citizens. In the summer of 1991, when I was paying a brief visit to friends and informants in the Huallaga Valley of Peru, an area that produces about two-thirds of the world's cocaine, two young Englishmen came to the city of Tingo María to visit the Cueva de la Lechuzas cave, which is known for its variety of birds. The two foreigners, who were equipped with powerful binoculars to watch exotic and rare birds and cameras to record their expedition, were walking in downtown Tingo María. Apparently, they were suspected of being U.S. Drug Enforcement or CIA agents. Two informants claimed to have seen a large group of men take them against their will. Six months later, one of the informants wrote that the two missing men were feared dead. Allegedly, Shining Path guerrillas were responsible for the deaths.

In another instance in Bolivia in 1986, four scientists were in the rain forests of Santa Cruz doing research on environmental and ecological problems. Drug traffickers attacked them because they were perceived as a threat. In the attack, three of the four scientists were shot to death; one escaped, hid in the bush for sixteen hours, and was rescued by a private plane (Malamud 1992:51).

Upon completion of fieldwork, the native researcher has to be more careful in writing about everything he sees in the field than nonnative researchers. The native researcher may have to play down his data because he might feel intimidated or concerned about what might happen to his property, family, or his long-term relationship with his subjects. Playing down data may mean not being able to allude to important findings if those findings could effect vindictive actions from people who do not want their behavior scrutinized, much less written about. For instance, when I was doing research on cocaine in Peru, I could not write on the arms deals between drug traffickers and army officials because I was *warned* not to do so. The implicit rule in the underground economy (the use of the term underground in the cocaine industry must encompass more than just traffickers) is that "you have never seen what you have seen." Thus, intrinsic to the politics of fieldwork (Punch 1986) is also maintaining the researcher's safety, not just protecting informants or satisfying funding sources.

Still Photography in Fieldwork

In ethnographic fieldwork, achieving rapport with the subjects is a long and constant process of adjustment to a social reality that might be totally alien to most researchers, especially to mainstream sociologists. Although today an increasing number of social researchers are doing ethnography, and although many nonacademic positions demand that social scientists be trained in ethnography, participant-observation is still more a part of anthropology than it is of any other discipline. Some anthropologists claim that photography has not gone farther than attesting to the researcher's presence in the field, and its use is confined to text illustrations (Homiak 1990); however, anthropology and sociology have used photography since their beginnings (Harper 1987:1).

Recently, social researchers have used still photography to gather information on human behavior to help them penetrate their subjects' or informants' worlds. The use of the camera in fieldwork affects the behavior of both subjects and the researcher. The researcher must be sensitive to moral and ethical constraints, and he or she must adjust to the conditions established on the grounds of how others perceive him or her (Goffman 1967:49). The camera changes the image of the researcher in the minds of others, and not always in the same way, depending upon the setting. The camera becomes a kind of obstacle that curtails interaction with the subject. In order to surmount this barrier, the researcher must be patient and tactful.

Two basic aspects of still photography in field research merit consideration here: the camera in the hands of the native or the nonnative, and the use of instant film during fieldwork.[5] Photographs enhance the engagement of subjects (Silvers 1988:183), accelerate entrée into their worlds (Collier and Collier 1986:16), and enable or force the researcher to experience the surrounding world through his five senses.

The use of the camera in social research, particularly if the researcher has been a serious photographer before becoming a social scientist, may present minor problems. His attitude may be that the camera and related equipment are as important to him as a brush is to the painter, or a scalpel to a surgeon. Ethnographers who use photography may often consider that their ability to collect good photographic information depends as much on the equipment, film speed, and good resolution as on their talent. My experience is that this is not the case. I have found that photographic sophistication, in many cases, hinders rapport with subjects and creates a communication barrier. A camera with a good normal 50mm lens and one short focal length lens is appropriate working equipment. This basic gear allows or forces one to come close to the subjects. Medium and long telephoto lenses, to the contrary, entice the researcher to "steal images."

People always look more askance at natives who walk around taking pictures and asking questions than they do at foreigners in the same situation. A camera in the hands of a foreigner is not new to the indigenous peasants. They seem to assume that every technological gadget is the creation and part of the foreigner's cultural garb. Conversely, people's attitudes toward a native holding a camera or taking pictures of them or their culture are totally different. For instance, it is a common practice to ask the native researcher to quote his fee for taking pictures. Indigenous and native people cooperate more with foreigners because they believe that they will get something in exchange for their cooperation. The odds of making people suspicious, especially field gatekeepers, are against the native. At times, the total stranger is even expected to photograph some aspects of the material culture, or the people's behavior.

For the subject and researcher to interact with each other, however, much more than academic training is required. What is necessary is what Latin Americans call *don de gente* or *don de persona* (a personal touch). A photojournalist or a commercial photographer may have a high degree of motivation, as well as a keen sense of light, composition, timing, and an idea of the picture editor's needs or taste, all of which come from training and experience. But the *don de gente* that the social observer needs, as Harris and Sartor (1984:3) put so clearly, "is not a science and cannot be taught. For those who have it, [it] is a gift that comes naturally, from within." For the researcher this gift is only part of the image perceived by subjects;

the other part may be his camera hanging around his neck or stored in his gadget bag, for being aware of his equipment and photographic interest will inevitably show during his interactions.

Although for the subjects the camera and the researcher may be considered as a single unit, in practice, photography must not be the researcher's main concern; rather it must be a by-product of his activities in a given setting and social environment. In the summer of 1991 I hiked for a few hours to visit two elderly peasant women who had agreed to provide detailed information on *chuchuncuy* (described in the Introduction). I deliberately asked a twenty-year-old girl, who knew the highlands well, to be my companion for the day. Upon our arrival at the cluster of houses and huts where the elderly women lived, some people came out of their houses to greet us; others just looked at me and asked my companion about my identity and interest, all of which I understood. When we arrived at the house, the two informants were about to leave for the field and were surprised to see me sooner than the approximate day we had set for the interview. I chose to go early because I wanted the interview to be as spontaneous as possible. I perceived that the camera hanging on my shoulder made them feel uncomfortable.

I put the camera away and tried to converse with the two elderly women and two other younger women who were part of the extended family. As I tried to focus my conversation on the topic on which we had agreed, I could see them staring at my canvas case. They thought that the camera was surreptitiously taking pictures of them of its own accord. Their reaction to my explanation of the camera's operations was that "if decades ago *pishtakos* (mythical men who killed people for human fat) could make their knives fly right to the neck of the victims from great distances, and if the planes today fly over such high mountains, why not think of a camera seeing through a few layers of canvas." As they talked about the carnival during their youth, they cooked two cuys for lunch and, later in the afternoon, they brewed a mix of aromatic herbs which we had with the crackers that I had brought from town. When I was about to leave they complained that I had not taken pictures of them. I took this opportunity to photograph the house including the inside of the kitchen. Had I set out to photograph them at the beginning, they probably would have been more defensive than they subsequently were.

Instant Film as a Research Aide

The use of instant positive film can serve three purposes. First and foremost, it can be used for exposure and composition tests. Second, it eases entrée to and rapport with some groups and persons. Third, the exposure tests may lead to conversations and elicit information on events or occasions that otherwise may be difficult or impossible to obtain. (The instant film sheets can be exposed with many medium format cameras available to the consumer.)[6] During the planning period for my fieldtrip to Bolivia and Peru that took place in the summer of 1990, I debated for many weeks what type of equipment and film to take to the field. I weighed the advantages and disadvantages of small and medium format cameras, and I decided to take my medium format equipment only because it accepted Polaroid film magazines.[7] However, the use of the instant print film went much further than I had expected. The advantages of lugging medium format equipment to the field were delivery of instant prints and the emotional rewards for both the researcher and the subjects; in many cases, the instant pictures were used as token compensation for the subjects' participation in a research project.

In some situations the use of this type of film may elicit interesting themes and revealing points of view. In Bolivia, the Parque Cementerio of Oruro (a small square beside the cemetery) is well known for its *llatiris* (sages). In this plaza many llatiris sit on the park benches with their decks of cards, coca leaf bags, or, occasionally, fresh eggs in their hands. Patients and clients come to see the llatiris for consultation about health conditions and business or personal concerns. I approached one of the llatiris and aimed my camera, mounted with a medium telephoto lens, at him. The llatiri's reaction to my wanting to photograph him was an emphatic, "You probably are a *kharisiri*."[8]

To gain the llatiri's confidence, and to encourage him to elaborate on the kharisiri myth, I took an instant picture of him and gave it to him. He commented on the picture itself and volunteered his criticism on instant prints. "I have seen many instant print cameras. In fact, one of my clients here in the city has one," he said. "The reason why I did not believe that your camera was such was because all instant cameras I have seen eject the exposed film and yours does not," he added. "This picture is much sharper than the many I have seen, but it seems rather smaller than the ones taken with cameras that eject the exposed film," he concluded. He invited me to sit on the bench, got ready to read his cards for me in exchange for the instant picture, and then he explained to me the myth of kharisiri.[9]

Although in tourist areas indigenous people are somewhat familiar with such items as cameras and binoculars, the challenge is to gain rapport with subjects and to succeed in convincing them to accept that the researcher is not an aggressor.[10] Techniques and strategies for approaching and winning informants may change with the conditions in the field, as well as the researcher's photographic interest. Some researchers may pay their subjects to be informants and to be photographed. Others may use their client-friend relationship to achieve long-term research projects (Harper 1987). The fact is that in order to observe and photograph subjects the researcher must accept some implicit, or explicit, conditions found in the field or established by informants or gatekeepers. One of these conditions is that people always expect something in exchange for sharing their personal or group experience. The explanation of doing research to enhance the subjects' human conditions, a classic cliché, is a white lie that native researchers cannot afford to overuse because, unlike nonnative researchers, they are not totally disconnected from the social reality they are researching.

Many experienced professional photographers, especially freelancers who cannot afford to budget cash outlays to pay their subjects in the field, carry with them notions such as needles, cheap pens, and costume jewelry or candies to pass out to people. Others change a few dollars into national currency in denominations of ten, fifty, or one-hundred bills or coins. Depending on the exchange rate these bills may be worth as little as one cent on the dollar. For instance, in the summer of 1992 there was an American freelance photographer who had been in Ecuador for more than six months. Every time he took pictures of children and the elderly, which seemed to be his particular interest, he would give them a few candies or fifty or one-hundred-sucre bills (100 sucres was equivalent to U.S.$.06). When people would not accept a fifty-sucre bill he would add another fifty or a few candies. In any case, he would pay his subjects after he had photographed them, which gave the subjects no leverage to negotiate a better treatment for their cooperation with the photographer.

My practice has been to give my subjects instant color prints. This approach, however advantageous as it may sound, presents problems. The high cost of instant film is prohibitive. A pack of sixteen sheets of film costs over U.S.$15 and, if bought outside the United States, it may go for as high as U.S.$40 per pack. That is, in some cases, the cost of instant film alone may be higher or as high as the cost of airfare to the field. Academics cannot afford to spend U.S.$500 to U.S.$700 on instant film during each extended fieldtrip, unless they are supported by a grant that can allow budgeting such an expense. Once the researcher is in the field, on the one hand, even a small fee charged to informants for instant prints would be more than most could afford, and the researcher would appear as though he were engaged in a profit-making enterprise. On the other hand, not giving free instant prints could cause subjects to become disgruntled; then, of course, there are sometimes people who have little or nothing to do with the project who would take advantage of the occasion to get a free photograph. For instance, in a small town a policeman requested that I take group and personal pictures of his family. Half a pack of film went to satisfy this request, which caused resentment among other people who, when they saw me taking pictures of natives and their behavior, would say that I was wasting film on "unimportant things."

Polaroid instant black-and-white film can be a substitute for a portable darkroom in order to make proofs with which to interview in the field, confirm appropriate exposure and composition, and yield good-quality negatives with a simple one-step development. Giving an instant print to subjects can lead to spontaneous conversations about the contents of the picture, or make up for the oversight of important aspects of the culture, or even make the researcher realize that people in advanced societies are poor observers. In contrast, people in underdeveloped countries must be diligent observers of their surroundings or else perish (Collier and Collier 1986:6). A shepherd boy, before he herds his flock to a grazing land away from home, looks up to the sky to see the direction of the clouds in order to forecast weather conditions; a summer flood could kill his lamb. Or, if a peasant is working out in the field and on a cloudy day cannot see the position of the sun to tell the time, he may use other methods to do so; such a method might be noticing the time of day (previously noted and therefore expected) for the arrival or departure of an airliner above his community.

The use of the instant Polaroid can also uncover facts about a subject's behavior, lifestyle or personal background. An old peasant man asked me to photograph him against the backdrop of his town. When I handed the small instant print to him, he went into his storage room and came out with an old sepia print of the town and a loupe to look at the Polaroid print. After inspecting the picture closely, he shut his doors and requested a retake of the picture. (My attitude while in the field is that film is the cheapest supply that one can carry, so I did not question this peasant's asking me to retake the photo.) I discovered that, in addition to being an extraordinary informant on the urbanization of the countryside, this peasant was a sort of repository of knowledge of the Andean culture. He was so immersed in our conversation that he showed me his faded picture taken while in service during the war between Peru and Ecuador in 1940.

At the end of his long lecture on the history of his town and other things Andean, which had been prompted by the instant print, he opened the door to his room, grabbed a big male cuy running about under his wooden bedstead, and gave it to me to take home. The reason for his requesting that I retake his photograph with the door of his room closed was that he did not want the photograph to reveal that he was sharing his room with his cuys. Had it not been for the peasant's request of me to photograph him, and the visually pleasing and mentally stimulating instant print, I would not have found this valuable informant.

When I visited Vicos, Peru,[11] in the summer of 1991, I met an elderly weaver whose kitchen satisfied all of my criteria for the use of space in the Andean household, including the traditional method of raising cuys in the kitchen. Examining my contact sheets, I was delighted to discover that the weaver was the same person whom John Collier had photographed several years ago (see Collier and Collier 1986:55). The contents of the two photographs of Julian and Rosa Tadeo speak for themselves about life in the Andes. By showing these photographs to the Tadeos or their relatives I was able to elicit information on many local, national social, and political events. Visual stimuli triggered recollections that might otherwise have been difficult or impossible to get. Methodologically, to conduct a scientifically sound study it would be necessary to collect data from the same sample at two different points in time. This would guarantee the objectivity of data collected through the use of photography in the same way it does for data collected in a more standard way through questionnaires.

Notes

Introduction

1. In the Andes it is common for people to share their experiences in traditional medicine voluntarily with one another. In June 1994 in the section that is known as a bus terminal of the city of Ibarra, Ecuador, I came in contact with a woman who had an open wound above her left eyebrow. A peddler who was selling *fritada* (fried pork) urged the woman to apply black cat's blood on the injury for one week.

2. During the Inca times a special class of women in the nobility memorized the *arawis*, passing them down to their eldest children with great accuracy. In each *panaca* (something like an extended family), there were four or five *arawicos* (those who chanted *arawis*) who memorialized the deeds of the dead kings. Metraux (1969:41) relates that the arawi celebrating the power and conquest of the Incas was heard for the last time in Cuzco in 1616. It is unclear how this erotic play is associated with the *arawi* as an oral chronicle.

3. Personal communication with Roberto Moncayo during a week's stay at his farm, May 22–28, 1994.

4. Reciprocities are mechanisms of mutual or cooperative interchange characteristic of the nonmonetary economic systems that function in the Andes outside of, but not isolated from, the national monetary systems (Mayer 1974:13).

1: From Household Animal to Market Commodity

1. Information provided by Elizabeth Rico of Mejocuy, Bolivia, and Julio Gamarra of Proyecto Baños del Inca, Cajamarca, Peru (personal communication, November 10, 1993).

2. Recent microbiological research questions whether the guinea pig

is a rodent. See Graur, Hide, and Wen-Hsing Li (1991: 649–651). *Nature Magazine*

3. Cuy, a Spanish word according to Parker and Chavez (1976:233), is part of many word combinations. For instance, in the word *cuycocha*, cuy is combined with cocha, also a Quechua word, to make "lake cuy."

4. Personal communication with agronomists Marco Zaldívar and Lilia Chauca, Lima, Peru, June 28, 1990.

5. The Ministerio de Agricultura y Ganadería (MAG) reports that an estimated 10 million cuys come from household producers in the highlands. This estimation does not include cuys raised on the coast or in the rain forests.

6. Personal communication with Alberto Caycedo, Pasto, Nariño, June 14, 1994.

7. The cuy is to the highlands what the coca leaf is to the rain forests. Coca leaves are picked every sixty-five to seventy days.

8. Researchers, scientists, and cuy farmers use the term criollo to mean native or indigenous. This meaning is quite different from the use of the word criollo in Latin American social history. Criollo was the word used to describe the children of European couples, especially Spaniards, born in America.

9. This information, provided by Roberto Moncayo of Auquicuy, Ecuador (personal communication 1993), disproves the National Research Council's (1991:245) claim that a farmer starting with one male and ten females could see his flock grow to 3,000 animals in one year.

10. Some people in some areas of Puno believe that cuys, because they eat day and night, consume feed that otherwise would be available to other animals such as llama, cattle, and sheep.

11. Information provided by Alberto Caycedo and Kelvi Heredia (personal communication, June 13, 1994, Pasto, Colombia).

12. Zaldívar and Chauca (personal communication) claim that there has been only one case in Huancayo, Peru, in which a breeder produced a cuy of almost 3 kilos.

13. Personal communication with Lilia Chauca, November 10, 1993, Riobamba, Chimbozaro, Ecuador.

14. Koeslag 1989. (ILEIA), (April 1989), vol. 5, no. 1.

15. Information in this paragraph comes from a proposal for research to be done with three Colombian scholars at the Universidad de Nariño.

16. In Latin America, mestizo and Indian are two very complex terms. Definitions of these words are influenced more by the Andean people's exposure to Western culture than by any substantive ethnic differences. Indians can be defined as groups of native people related by common descent and having the same ethnic characteristics. An Indian

then would be of the ethnic group that has more or less maintained certain physical traits as well as social, religious, and linguistic traditions transmitted from older generations. In this sense, there are no pure Indians in the Andes. In fact, most "Indians" are "non-Indians," and the group includes many European groups absorbed by the Andean traditional culture. Sociologically, the term "Indians" is used to define the poorest group of the peasantry who have some of the same characteristics, such as language, beliefs, and folk practices (Spalding 1974:147).

17. Rios-Reategui (1978:6) reports that there are 25,000 plants of coca in one hectare of land. Government officials and academics, however, agree that in one hectare of land there are only 10,000 plants of coca, for the distance from one plant to another is about one meter.

2: The Cuy as Food and Symbolic Social Binder

1. For a detailed analysis of the complexities of food in society see Goody (1982).

2. For a systematic and detailed discussion of cooking, culinary practices, and the meaning of food see Goody (1982). See also Leach (1976:29) and Douglas (1975:249–275).

3. For instance, after storing seed for the next planting season, families preserve tubers such as potatoes and ocas using the millenarian tradition of freezing and dehydrating. See Catherine J. Allen (1988:74) and Ana Maria Fries (1989:37).

4. Social class is a designation for a large group of people within a system of social stratification who have a similar socioeconomic status in relation to other segments of their society or community. Social differentiation is a process by which different statuses, roles, and groups develop or persist within a society, which changes over time with the changes in traditions and values.

5. *Chanka* in Quechua means legs; therefore, *chanka de conejo* would be translated as cuy legs.

6. For a more detailed description of the different cuy dishes and recipes in Ecuador and Peru see Archetti (1992) and Ayala-Loayza (1989), respectively.

7. Huaraz is the administrative and financial seat for the Valley of Huaylas and the capital of the Department (state) of Ancash. This city was devastated by an earthquake in 1970, which killed at least fifty thousand people. After the earthquake the government built a paved road and an airport that connected this city to Lima. Modern and faster means of transportation have brought about new behaviors and caused changes in many traditions and customs, including those surrounding food.

3: The Cuy in Andean Medicine

1. Barahona (1982:151), based on his observation of four healers in a highland community in Ecuador, argues that the healer who rubs a patient with cuy is not a curandero but a *sobador de cuy*.

2. I should emphasize that during my four summers of fieldwork some curanderos allowed me to observe them while others were reticent to provide any information, for they claimed that their skill was a god-given gift or power bestowed by the supernatural whose method and procedure could not be discussed.

3. The susto is a socially constructed illness in which the human body is divided into concrete mass and ethereal or intangible substance. The intangible substance may become detached or may become a captive of supernatural forces (Rubel, O'Neal, and Collado-Ardon 1984:8) or struggles to become detached to wander around as a punishment for the sins of the person. For instance, in some communities in the highlands of Peru, people call women who have, or had, sexual intercourse with a priest *mulas*. They believe that the soul of the mula leaves the body when, at midnight, the devil shows at the door of the mula's house. The mula comes out at the command (whistle) of the devil (priest), who rides on her along narrow trails and gorges. At the end the devil ties his mula to a thorny bush and goes back to his convent or church. Or, in some instances, the mula is left wandering around the open field. People, especially children who spot the mula wandering around, follow her closely and cover her footprint with a slate. When they pick up the slate after a few minutes they believe they will see a fresh horseshoe print.

4. Elsewhere shoga or shogay is known as *shokma* (Valencia-Ponce 1975:89) and is a therapy that consists in bathing the patient in water that contains flowers, leaves, and herbs to cure *susto* (fright).

5. *Salasacas* do not call the earth *pacha mama* as other people in Bolivia and Peru do.

6. This particular curandero's healing sessions always take place late in the evenings or during the night. His only method of healing is special prayers guided by the magical power of the coca leaf. He is an eighty-year-old man who claims to have been resuscitated and given powers to cure in return for his life. Unlike urban curanderos, he does not have a fixed fee for his services. He accepts whatever the patient can afford that, at times, is no more than half a dozen fresh eggs or a small sackful of corn ears or a few cents (the new Peruvian Sol is equivalent to about U.S.$.08) from those who can pay in cash. On my field trip of December 1992 I planned to photograph this curandero. Unfortunately, he died three days before I arrived in the community.

4: The Cuy in Andean Ideology, Religion, and Belief

1. During colonial times, this province was part of the territory known as Conchucos, which the conquistadors named after a *chuco* (Quechua dialect for hat) that the Indians wore. Thus, according to Garcilaso de la Vega (1953), "conchucos" means Indians wearing chucos.

2. For a detailed description and analysis of a similar religious festivity that takes place in Otuzco, in northern Peru, during which people slaughter cuys, see Robert Smith (1975).

3. For a good discussion of the cultural role of the festivities of the patron saints in Lima see Marzal (1988:85–123).

4. Bergson (1914:3). *An Essay on the Meaning of the Comic* (New York: The Macmillan Company, 1914), p. 3.

5. For a detailed discussion of ideology, rituals, and domination in northern Ecuador see Crain (1989: 169–209).

6. Chunks of roasted cuy are invariably in every chiri uchu meal. On the main day of Pentecost, a local baker roasted as many as 300 cuys for the other three carguyocs and private families. Depending on the host's or the vendor's preference and/or availability of food supply, the rest of the ingredients may vary.

7. Because of the unofficial nature of the festivity, any or all of the dates of Corpus Christi can be changed. For instance, in 1992 the Chishi Octava that was programmed for July 5 was moved forward to July 12 because of the general elections held on the former day.

8. Sarzosa and Leon (1991:129) conclude that Salasaca people maintain their culture and that festivities are important for transmitting customs and traditions to younger generations. Given the changes that they are experiencing, this conclusion may not present an accurate picture of the Salasacas. My observation is that younger generations do not observe their rituals as older people do. They rarely come by to the alcalde's house to watch the rituals or eat or drink with the rest of the people. They are busier watching television, playing volleyball, or just hanging out in the nearby town.

9. From Guerrero Arias (1991), p. 92.

10. Some of the mountains that are believed to be the dwellings for the ancestors are also archaeological sites.

5: The Future of the Cuy Economy

1. Name and location of this South American ethnic restaurant is not given here at the request of the owner.

2. As Enrique Mayer (personal communication) remarked, it would

not be surprising to see in the future fast-food franchises where KFC might stand for Kentucky Fried Cuy.

Appendix

1. Immersion implies the fieldworker's total absorption by the foreign culture in all its broad context; therefore, it may not apply to the native researcher.

2. The Andes presents a heterogeneous natural and human ecology. It is more diverse than we think it is. There are variations in traditions, habits, and language, which, added to geographical differences, mold dozens of distinct small nations clustered in dissimilar ecozones. For example, while I may be viewed as a native Peruvian in my home state (Región Chavín), I may not be easily accepted in many parts of the Andes. Even my fluency in the native language and knowledge of the culture may not quite correlate with my personal presentation. It is rarely the case that people accept the native researcher as "one of them." On the contrary they may secretly try to foil the project after having agreed to cooperate with the study as I experienced during my dissertation research (Morales 1989:175).

3. For instance, Latin Americans, especially Andeans, often express their animadversion to the fact that the natives were conquered by the Spanish. "Had white people conquered us we would not be experiencing such a stagnant society," they say.

4. As a result of the foreign researcher's fieldwork, it is not uncommon, especially in Andean communities, to find people who have American and European *compadres* (spiritual relatives). It is interesting to see that nonnative researchers take this relationship seriously. For instance, an American anthropologist who visits Ecuador and southern Colombia frequently helps her compadres with the medical expenses of her godchild.

5. Technical aspects of still photography have been published extensively. Indeed, there are a number of manuals and how-to books from which anyone interested in still photography can get information. The best guide that I know of is the pocket-sized booklet published by the National Geographic Society. But the best short course in photography is the manual that comes packaged with the camera.

6. Polaroid has put on the market a compact instant print camera that takes ten $2\frac{1}{4}$ x $3\frac{3}{4}$ pictures. The camera weighs only 26 ounces and measures $4\frac{1}{8}$ x $4\frac{3}{8}$ x 7 inches when open for viewing and exposing the film. Its suggested retail price in the United States is $125, which at discount camera stores in New York can be purchased for under $100.

7. Thirty-five-millimeter and smaller cameras are defined as small

format cameras. Medium format cameras are the ones that take 120–220 and 70 mm film and sheet film up to 9 cm x 12 cm.

8. In Bolivian Andean folklore, kharisiri is a monk who during the months of July and August leaves his monastery for the countryside to look for human fat to make chrism (oil that is consecrated and then used in various sacraments of the Roman Catholic church, such as baptism and confirmation). A lay-friar carrying tin boxes to deposit the human fat goes along with the kharisiri monk. The wicked monk identifies his victim; he pampers him and numbs him with a strong narcotic, and then he makes a small incision in the right side of the victim's abdomen to extract fat from the body. Once he draws the amount of fat he needs, the monk applies a magic medicine to the cut and goes back to his monastery. When the victim regains his conscious state, he realizes that the pain he feels on his stomach and the scar are evidence of having been victimized by the kharisiri; he knows that his chances of healing are very slight. He agonizes for many weeks and dies. In some areas of Cochabamba, Bolivia, people claim that there are certain powers that one can use against the kharisiri. One power entails carrying a sewing needle. Once one perceives the presence of a kharisiri one sticks the needle into the ground and urinates, making a circle around the needle. This temporarily distracts the kharisiri so that the victim can run away. Some llatiris claim that they actually infuse fat into the kharisiri victim's body. They claim that the most common method is to heat up black lamb's fresh skin over the steam of boiling chuño (dehydrated potato), then place it on the wound for as many times as it is needed to replace the fat extracted from the body. The kharisiri seems to be a mythical explanation of Spanish greed, as well as of exploitation and decimation of the native population during the colonial period.

9. This kharisiri folk myth in Bolivia is known as pishtaco in the highlands of Peru. The difference is that the pishtako actually kills his victims to take the fatty parts of the human body.

10. For a good discussion of the subjects' perception of the photographer as an aggressor see Bill Jay, "The Photographer as Aggressor" in David Featherstone, editor, Observations: Essays on Documentary Photography (San Francisco: The Friends of Photography, 1984), 6–23.

11. Vicos, a former hacienda in the northeastern Andes of Peru, where Cornell University had a research project for many years, is now a legally organized community. For a visual glimpse of Vicos in the early 1950s see Collier (1967) and Collier and Collier (1986:50–55).

Bibliography

Alberti, Giorgio, and Enrique Mayer, eds.

    1974   *Reciprocidad e Intercambio en los Andes Peruanos* Lima, Perú: Instituto de Estudios Peruanos, 1974.

Aliaga-Rodríguez, Luis.

    1989   "Sistemas de Crianza de Cuyes en Pequeñas Fincas." *Curso Latino Americano Sobre Producción de Cuyes.* Lima, Perú: Estación Experimental Agropecuaria y Agroindustrial.

Allen, Catherine J.

    1988   *The Hold Life Has: Coca and Cultural Identity in an Andean Community.* Washington, D.C.: Smithsonian Institution Press.

Archetti, Eduardo

    1992   *El Mundo Social y Simbólico del Cuy.* Quito, Ecuador: Centro de Planificación y Estudios Sociales.

Ayala-Loayza, Juan Luis

    1990   *Horticultura y Cria del Cuy.* Lima, Perú: Kollao Editorial.

Balladelli, Pier P.

    1990   *Entre lo Mágico y lo Natural: La Medicina Indígena.* Quito, Ecuador: Ediciones Abya-Yala.

Barahona, Claudio

    1982   "La Soba de Cuy." In Sanchez-Parga, José, ed. *Política de Salud y Comunidad Andina.* Quito, Ecuador: Centro Andino de Acción Popular, pp. 141–151.

Bastien, Joseph W.

    1985   *Mountain of the Condor: Metaphor and Ritual in an Andean Ayllu.* Prospect Heights, IL: Waveland Press.

    1987   *Healers of the Andes: Kallawaya Herbalists and Their Medicinal Plants.* Salt Lake City: University of Utah Press.

Bennett, Wendell C., and Junius Bird.
  1949   *Andean Culture History.* New York: American Museum of Natural
          History.
Berger, John, and Jean Mohr
  1982   *Another Way of Telling.* New York: Pantheon Books.
Berger, Peter L., and Thomas Luckmann
  1967   *The Construction of Reality.* New York: Doubleday.
Bergson, Henry
  1914   *Laughter: An Essay on the Meaning of the Comic.* London: Macmillan.
Bolton, Ralph.
  1979   "Guinea Pigs, Protein, and Ritual." *Ethnology* 18:229–52.
Botero, Luis Fernando, ed.
  1991   *Compadres y Priostes: La fiesta andina como epacio de memoria y resistencia
          cultural.* Quito, Ecuador: Ediciones Abya-yala.
Brundage, Burr Cartwright
  1967   *Lords of Cuzco: A History and Description of the Inca People in their Final Days.*
          Norman: The University of Oklahoma Press.
Burbano, Segundo
  1994   "La Cultura Popular del Cuy." M. A. Thesis, Universidad de
          Nariño, Pasto, Colombia.
Cain, Diana
  1989   "Living With 'Our Silent Brothers.'" *The Officer Paper,* March
          1989.
Calderola, Victor
  1985   "Visual Contexts: A Photographic Research Method in An-
          thropology." *Studies in Visual Communication,* 11:33–55.
Campaña, Victor A.
  1991   *Fiesta y Poder: La Celebración de Rey de Reyes en Riobamba.* Quito, Ecua-
          dor: Ediciones Abya-Yala.
Caycedo, Alberto
  1984   "Edad Optima de Sacrificio y Preparación de la Canal." *Primer
          Curso sobre Producción de Cuyes.* Pasto, Colombia: Universidad de
          Nariño, Facultad de Zootecnia, Agosto 13–17, 1984.
  1988   *Alimentación y Sanidad del Cuy.* Popayán, Colombia: Asesorias y Fo-
          mento Socioeconomico.
  1993   *Linea de Investigación en Cuyes y sus Alcances en la Tecnificación de la Explota-
          ción.* Pasto, Colombia: Universidad de Nariño.
Centro Interamericano de Artesanias y Artes Populares (CIDAP)
  1986   *La Cultura Popular en el Ecuador Tomo II Cotopaxi.* Quito, Ecuador:
          CIDAP.
  1989   *La Cultura Popular en el Ecuador Tomo V Imbabura.* Quito, Ecuador:
          CIDAP.

Charbonneau, Robert

    1988   "Fiesta for Six: One Guinea Pig . . . and We'll All Be Full." *The International Development Research Center (IDRC) Reports*, vol. 17, no. 3 (July). Ottawa, Canada: IDRC, pp. 6–7.

Chauca, Lilia

    1989   "Necesidades Nutritivas de Cuyes." *Curso Latino Americano Sobre la Producción de Cuyes.* Lima, Perú: Instituto Nacional de Investigación Agraria y Agroindustrial.

    1993a *Experiencias en el Perú en la Producción de Cuyes.* Lima, Perú: Instituto Nacional de Investigación Agraria.

    1993b "Nutrición y Alimentación de Cuyes." Paper presented at IV Congreso Latinoamericano de Cuyecultura, Riobamba, Ecuador.

Chauca, Lilia, and Marco Zaldivar

    1989a "Consideraciones Generales para la Instalación de una Granja de Cuyes." *Curso Latino Americano Sobre la Producción de Cuyes.* Lima, Perú: Instituto Nacional de Investigación Agraria y Agroindustrial.

    1989b *Mejora tu Producción de Cuyes.* Lima, Perú: Instituto Nacional de Investigación Agraria y Agroindustrial.

Clay, Jason

    1989   "Epilogue: The Ethnic Future of Nations." *Third World Quarterly* 11(4): 223–233.

Collier, John, Jr.

    1967   *Visual Anthropology: Photography as a Research Method.* New York: Holt, Rinehart and Winston.

Collier, John, and Malcolm Collier.

    1986   *Visual Anthropology: Photography as a Research Method.* Albuquerque: University of New Mexico Press.

Convenio de Desarrollo Bélgica-Ecuador

    1991   *Proyecto de Desarrollo Comunal Palmira: Instrumento Técnico.* Quito, Ecuador: Embajada Bélgica.

Crain, Mary M.

    1989   *Ritual, Memoria Popular y Proceso Político en la Sierra Ecuatoriana.* Quito, Ecuador: Corporación Editora Nacional y Ediciones Abya-Yala.

de la Vega, Garcilaso

    1953   *Comentarios Reales de los Incas.* Mexico: Publicaciones de la Universidad de Puebla.

De Soto, Hernando

    1989   *The Other Path: The Invisible Revolution in the Third World.* New York: Harper and Row Publishers.

Detjen, Jim

    1991   "The Little Lost Guinea Pig: Did it Go in the Wrong Genetic Box?" *The Philadelphia Inquirer*, 20 June, p. A1.

Douglas, Mary

    1975   *Implicit Meanings*. London: Routlege and Kegan.

Elliott, Robert C.

    1960   *The Power of Satire: Magic, Ritual, Art*. Princeton: Princeton University Press.

Escobar, Gabriel, and Gloria Escobar

    1976   "Observaciones Etnográficas sobre la Crianza y los Usos del Cuy en la Región del Cuzco." *Antropología Andina* 1–2: 34–49.

Featherstone, David, ed.

    1984   *Observations: Essays on Documentary Photography*. Carmel, CA.: The Friends of Photography.

Fiddes, Nick

    1991   *Meat: A Natural Symbol*. New York: Routledge, 1991.

Finerman, Ruthbeth

    1989   "The Forgotten Healers: Women as Family Healers in an Andean Indian Community." In *Women as Healers: Cross-Cultural Perspectives*, edited by Carol Shepherd McClain. New Brunswick: Rutgers University Press.

Foster, Nelson, and Linda S. Cordell, eds.

    1992   *Chilies to Chocolate: Food the Americas Gave the World*. Tucson: University of Arizona Press.

Foster, Nelson, Thayer Scudder, Elizabeth Olson, and Robert Kemper, eds.

    1979   *Long-Term Field Research in Social Anthropology*. New York: Academic Press.

Fries, Ana Maria

    1989   *Puna, Qheswa, Yunga: El hombre y su medio en Q'ero*. Lima: Banco Central de Reserva del Perú.

Gade, Daniel W.

    1967   "The Guinea Pig in Andean Folk Culture." *The Geographical Review* 57:213–224.

Gans, Herbert J.

    1986   "Participant Observer as a Human Being: Observation on the Personal Aspects of Fieldwork." In Robert G. Burgess, *Field Research: a Sourcebook and Field Manual*. Winchester, MA: Allen and Unwin, Inc.

Goffman, Irving

    1967   *Interaction Ritual: Essays On Face-to-Face Behavior*. New York: Anchor Books.

Goody, Jack

    1982   *Cooking, Cuisine and Class: A Study in Comparative Sociology*. New York: Cambridge University Press.

Graur, Dan, Winston A. Hide, and Wen-Hsing Li

    1991   "Is the Guinea Pig a Rodent?" *Nature Magazine* 351 (June): 649–52.

Guaman Poma de Ayala, Felipe

    1980   *El Primer Nueva Crónica y Buen Gobierno*. Mexico: Siglo Veintiuno Editores. Originally published in 1615.

Guerrero-Arias, Edgar Patricio

    1991   "La Fiesta de la Mama Negra: Sincretismo, cambio cultural y resistencia," in *Compadres y Priostes: La fiesta andina como espacio de memoria y resistencia cultural*, edited by Luis Fernando Botero. Quito, Ecuador: Abya-Yala.

Guzman-Cabrera, Luis

    1968   "Periodo de Engorde en Cuyes y el Estudio Tecnológico de su Carne." Tesis, Universidad Agraria La Molina.

Guzman-Peredo, Miguel

    1985   *Prácticas Médicas en la América Antigua*. Mexico, D.F.: Ediciones Euroamericanas.

Hanke, Lewis

    1959   *Aristotle and the American Indians: A Study in Race Prejudice in the Modern World*. London: Hollis and Carter.

Harper, Douglas

    1987a "The Visual Ethnographic Narrative." *Visual Anthropology* 1:1–9.

    1987b *Working Knowledge*. Chicago: University of Chicago Press.

Harris, Alex, and Margaret Sartor, eds.

    1984   *Gertrude Bloom: Bearing Witness*. Chapel Hill: University of North Carolina Press.

Homiak, John P.

    1990   "Images on the Edge of the Text: Ethnographic Imaging and Views of the Anthropological Self." Paper presented at the 12th Annual Ohio University Film Conference, November 1990.

Howell, Nancy.

    1990   *Surviving Fieldwork: A Report of the Advisory Panel on Health and Safety in Fieldwork*. Washington: American Anthropological Association.

Isbell, Billie Jean

    1974   "Parentesco Andino y Reciprocidad Kuyaq: Los que nos Aman." In *Reciprocidad e Intercambio en los Andes Peruanos*, edited by

Giorgio Alberti and Enrique Mayer. Lima, Perú. Instituto de Estudios Peruanos, pp. 37–65.

1985 *To Defend Ourselves: Ecology and Ritual in an Andean Village.* Prospect Heights, IL: Waveland Press.

Koeslag, Johan H.

1989 "The Guinea Pig as Meat Producer." *Information Centre for Low External Input and Sustained Agriculture (ILEA) Newsletter* 5, pp. 22–23.

Lanning, Edward P.

1967 *Peru Before the Incas.* Englewood Cliffs, N.J.: Prentice Hall.

Leach, Edmund

1976 *Culture and Communication.* New York: Cambridge University Press.

Lee, Rensselaer W.

1989 *The White Labyrinth: Cocaine and Political Power.* New Brunswick, NJ: Transaction Publishers.

Leví-Strauss, Claude

1962 *Totemism.* Boston: Beacon Press.

Lira, Jorge A.

1985 *Medicina Andina: Farmacopea y Ritual.* Cusco, Perú: Centro de Estudios Rurales Andinos Bartolomé de las Casas.

Lobo, Susan.

1982 *A House of My Own.* Tucson: University of Arizona Press, 1982.

Lumbreras, Luis G.

1981 *Arqueología de la América Andina.* Lima, Perú: Editorial Milla Bartres.

1983 *Los Orígenes de la Civilización en el Perú.* Lima, Perú: Editorial Milla Bartres.

McCamant, John F.

1992 "Quinoa's Roundabout Journey to World Use." In *Chilies to Chocolate: Food the Americas Gave the World,* edited by Nelson Foster and Linda S. Cordell. Tucson: University of Arizona Press, pp. 123–141.

MAG (Ministerio de Agricultura y Ganadería)

1986 *Estudio Sobre la Situación Actual de la Crianza de Cuyes en la Región Interandina del Ecuador.* Quito, Ecuador: MAG, Junta Nacional del Acuerdo Cartagena, y Programa de la Naciones Unidas para el Desarrollo.

1991 "Fomentemos la Explotación de la Lombriz y Conservemos la Ecología." Quito, Ecuador: Dirección Nacional de Ganadería.

Malamud, Jaime

1992 *Smoke and Mirrors: The Paradox of the Drug Wars.* Boulder: Westview Press.

Margolis, Eric
    1990   "Visual Ethnography: Tools for Mapping the Aids Epidemic." *Journal of Contemporary Ethnography* 19 (October): 370–392.

Marquez-Zorrilla, Santiago
    1965   *Huari y Conchucos*. Lima, Perú: Imprenta "El Condor".

Marzal, Manuel M.
    1988   "La Fiesta Patronal Andina en la Ciudad de Lima." *Allpanchis* 31:85–123.

Mayer, Enrique
    1974   "Las Reglas de Juego en la Reciprocidad Andina." In *Reciprocidad e Intercambio en los Andes Peruanos*, edited by Giorgio Alberti and Enrique Mayer. Lima, Perú: Instituto de Estudios Peruanos, pp. 37–65.

Metraux, Alfred
    1969   *The History of the Incas*. New York: Pantheon Books.

Moncayo, Roberto
    1992a   "Aspectos de Manejo en la Producción Comercial de Cuyes." Paper presented at the III Congreso Andino de Cuyecultura, Lima, Perú.
    1992b   "Aspectos de la Comercialización en la Producción de Cuyes: Experiencias en el Ecuador." Paper presented at the III Congreso Andino de Cuyecultura, Lima, Perú.
    1992c   "Viabilidad y Rentabilidad en la Producción de Cuyes a Nivel Industrial." Paper presented at the 3d Congreso Andino de Cuyecultura, Lima, Perú.

Montenegro, Gerardo
    1993   "Estructura del Mercado del Cuy en el Departamento de Nariño, Colombia." *Memorias del IV Congreso Latinoamericano de Cuyecultura*, Riobamba, Ecuador 8–12 de Noviembre.

Morales, Edmundo
    1989   *Cocaine: White Gold Rush in Peru*. Tucson: University of Arizona Press.
    1994   "The Guinea Pig in Andean Economy: From Household Animal to Market Commodity." *Latin American Research Review* 3:129–143.

Muñoz, Laurentino
    1970   Historia Natural del Conejillo de Indias: de los Andes al Mundo. Popayán, Colombia: Talleres Editoriales del Departamento.

Navarro-Enriquez, José Gabriel
    1991   *La Pintura en el Ecuador del XVI at XIX*. Quito, Ecuador: Dinediciones.

NRC (National Research Council)

1989   *Lost Crops of the Incas.* Washington, D.C.: National Academy Press.

1991   *Microlivestock: Little-Known Small Animals with a Promising Economic Future.* Washington, D.C.: National Academy Press.

Parker, Gary, and Amancio Chavez

1976   *Diccionario Quechua Ancash-Huailas.* Lima, Perú: Instituto de Estudios Peruanos.

Pedersen, Duncan

1989   "Curanderos, Divinidades, Santos y Doctores: Elementos para el Analisis de los Sistemas Médicos." In *La Medicina Traditional en Sistemas Formales de Salud,* edited by Carles Roesch, Liesbeth van der Hoogte, and Jose María Tavares de Andrade. Cuzco, Perú: Centro de Medicina Andina, pp. 53–83.

Pozorski, Sheila Griffis, and Thomas George Pozorski

1987   *Early Settlement and Subsistence in Casma Valley, Peru.* Iowa City: University of Iowa Press.

Punch, Maurice

1986   *The Politics and Ethics of Fieldwork.* Beverly Hills: Sage Publications.

Rabinow, Paul

1977   *Reflections on Fieldwork in Morocco.* Berkeley: The University of California Press.

Reader, John

1988   *Man on Earth.* Austin: University of Texas Press.

Rios-Reategui, Raul

1978   "Problemática que Plantea el Cultivo de la Coca: Algunas Alternativas de Solución." Primer Forum sobre Recursos Naturales y Desarrollo Regional, Tingo María, Perú, Agosto.

Rouch, Jean

1975   "The Camera and Man." In *Principles of Visual Anthropology,* edited by Paul Hockings. The Hague: Mouton Publishers, pp. 83–102.

Rubel, Arthur J., Carl W. O'Neal, and Rolando Collado-Ardon

1984   *Susto: A Folk Illness.* Berkeley: University of California Press.

Ruiz-Calero, Oscar

n.d.   *El Secreto de los Andes.* La Paz, Bolivia: Editorial Imatgrom.

Salgado, Sebastiao

1986   *Other Americas.* New York: Pantheon Books.

Sallnow, Michael J.

1987   *Pilgrims of the Andes: Regional Cults in Cusco.* Washington: Smithsonian Institution.

Sanabria, Harry

1993   *The Coca Boom and Rural Social Change in Bolivia.* Ann Arbor: University of Michigan Press.

Saravia, Luis Miguel, and Rosa Sueiro Cabredo, eds.

1985   *Experiencias de Desarrollo Popular en el Campo de la Medicina Tradicional y Moderna*. Lima: Centro Amazónico de Antropología y Aplicación Práctica.

Sarzosa, Carmen, and Linda Leon

1991   "Corpus Christi en Salasaca." In *Compadres y Priostes: La Fiesta Adina como Epacio de Memoria y Resistencia Cultural*, edited by Luis Fernando Botero. Quito, Ecuador: Ediciones Abya-Yala, pp. 123–129.

Silvers, Ronald

1988   *A Pause on the Path*. Philadelphia: Temple University Press.

Smith, Carolyn, and William Kornblum, eds.

1989   *In the Field: Experiences in Field Research*. New York: Praeger Publishers.

Smith, Robert J.

1975   *The Arts of the Festival As Exemplified by the Fiesta to the Patroness of Otuzco: La Virgen de la Puerta*. Lawrence, Kansas: University of Kansas Publication in Anthropology, no. 6.

Spalding, Karen

1974   *De Indio a Campecino: cambios en la estructura social del Perú colonial*. Lima, Perú: Instituto de Estudios Peruanos.

Stahl, Peter, and Presley Norton

1984   "Animales Domésticos y las Implicaciones del Intercambio Precolombino desde Salango, Ecuador." *Miscelanea Antropológica Ecuatoriana* 4:83–96.

Stoller, Paul

1989   *The Taste of Ethnographic Things*. Philadelphia: University of Pennsylvania Press.

Thurner, Mark

1993   "Peasant Politics and Andean Haciendas in the Transition to Capitalism: An Ethnographic History." *Latin America Research Review* 28:41–82.

Tyler, S. Lyman

1988   *Two Worlds: The Indian Encounter with the European 1492–1509*. Salt Lake City: University of Utah Press.

Valencia-Ponce, Oscar

1975   *Hampicamayoc: Medicina Folklórica y su Substrato Aborigen en el Perú*. Lima: Universidad Nacional Mayor de San Marcos.

Van Maanen, John

1984   *Tales of the Field*. Chicago: University of Chicago Press.

Vargas, José María

1970   *Miguel de Santiago: Su Vida y su Obra*. Quito, Ecuador: Editorial Santo Domingo.

Weismantel, Mary J.

   1988   *Food, Gender, and Poverty in the Ecuadorian Andes.* Philadelphia: University of Pennsylvania Press.

Whyte, William F.

   1984   *Learning from the Field: A Guide from Experience.* Beverly Hills: Sage Publications.

Williams, Terry M.

   1989   *The Cocaine Kids: The Inside Story of a Teenage Drug Ring.* Reading, Ma.: Addison-Wesley Publishing Co.

Zaldivar-Abanto, Marco

   1968   "Sistemas de conservación de la carne de cuy." Lima, Perú: Ministerio de Agricultura, Dirección General de Investigación Agraria, Estación Experimental La Molina.

Index

About the Author

Edmundo Morales, born in the small town of Llamellín, Ancash, Peru, teaches sociology at West Chester University in Pennsylvania. He studied at Universidad National Mayor de San Marcos of Lima, Peru, New York University, and the Graduate School of the City University of New York where he received his Ph.D. in 1983. He is the author of *Cocaine: White Gold Rush in Peru* (also published by the University of Arizona Press) and several articles on cocaine and economic development in Peru. His current work in South America focuses on the role of Andean women in rural economic development and also on environmental education research in the Peruvian Amazon. He is also working on an ethnographic and photographic documentary on migrant workers in the mushroom industry in rural Pennsylvania. His photographs have been exhibited at the Museum of the City of New York and many libraries in the United States and Europe.

Library of Congress Cataloging-in-Publication Data

Morales, Edmundo, 1943–
    The guinea pig : healing, food, and ritual in the Andes /
Edmundo Morales.
        p. cm.
    Includes bibliographical references and index.
    Contents: From household animal to market commodity—The
cuy as food and symbolic social binder—The cuy in Andean
medicine—The cuy in Andean ideology, religion, and belief—The
future of the cuy economy.
    ISBN 0-8165-1479-8 (alk. paper).—
    ISBN 0-8165-1558-1 (pbk.: alk. paper)
    1. Indians of South America—Andes Region—Domestic animals.
2. Guinea pigs—Social aspects—Andes Region.   3. Guinea pigs—
Andes Region—History.   4. Indians of South America—Andes Region—Food.   5. Indians of South America—Andes Region—Economic conditions.
I. Title.
F2230.1.D65M67   1995   95-4343
338.1'7693234—dc20   CIP

British Library Cataloguing-in-Publication Data
A catalogue record for this book is available from the British Library.